Twayne's United States Authors Series

Sylvia E. Bowman, *Editor*

INDIANA UNIVERSITY

Lillian Smith

LILLIAN SMITH

By **LOUISE BLACKWELL**
Florida A. and M. University

and

FRANCES CLAY
Florida State University

(TUSAS) 187

Twayne Publishers, Inc.   ::   New York

To Our Mothers

GLADYS BLACKWELL SELLS AND ANNIE LEE CLAY

And to the Memory of

CAPTAIN DAVID WALKER CLAY, U.S.A.F.

(1919-1944)

Preface

FOR SOME THIRTY YEARS, until her death on September 28, 1966, Lillian Smith was in the mainstream of the New South group of Southern writers, a group that had its beginnings in 1886 with Henry W. Grady's speech, "The New South." Grady was pleading for economic cooperation between the North and South and for diversification of agriculture and development of natural resources in the South. Journalists, sociologists, and novelists took up Grady's theme, each giving his own ideas about *how* the South could be made new. In recent years, however, the "problem" of the Negro in the South has taken precedence over agricultural and industrial problems.

Lillian Smith was a boldly outspoken advocate of equality for all races, and particularly for the Negro in the United States. For eight years before the publication of her famous novel, *Strange Fruit* (1944), she had been writing and publishing her views on racial segregation, imperialism, religion, literature, and art. She was a person of many interests and varied talents, some of which were overlooked by both her friends and her enemies, who preferred to praise or blame her for her views on race relations.

One purpose of this study, therefore, is to introduce Miss Smith to the reader by outlining her life, beginning with her early years in Jasper, Florida, and Clayton, Georgia, and running through four years of preparation to become a concert pianist, three years of teaching in China, and some twenty years as director of a summer camp for girls, a period which overlapped with her thirty years as a writer. It is with her achievements as a writer, from 1936 to 1966, that this study is primarily concerned; and every effort has been made to collect and analyze all of Miss Smith's writings. These include numerous items in the "little" magazine, *South Today*, which she founded and edited; a series of newspaper columns for the *Chicago Defender*; two novels, *Strange Fruit* and *One Hour*; five nonfiction books; and a number of magazine articles.

Although her college education was limited to one year at Piedmont College in north Georgia and approximately one year at Teachers College, Columbia University, Miss Smith was an avid reader in various fields, including history, sociology, psychology, and literature. For ten years, beginning in the 1930's, she read widely and deeply in the areas of psychology and psychoanalysis. Thus all of her writings, fiction and nonfiction, reflect her interest in Freudian psychology. As this study shows, her works reveal her deep and constant concern for the dignity of all mankind. She not only criticized such things as racial segregation and McCarthyism, but she made suggestions for correction of such injustices. And she lived to see many corrective measures put into effect. Although it is difficult to measure the influence her works had on the changes that have been wrought in the United States, hers must be acknowledged as one of the strongest voices in this century in behalf of racial equality and social justice in the United States.

Our work in gathering information for this study was greatly facilitated by Miss Smith, who, even though she was seriously ill in 1965 and 1966, talked with us, made notes for us, and loaned us some of her files. We could not have asked for friendlier cooperation than Miss Smith gave us. We also wish to thank Miss Paula Snelling, a close friend of Miss Smith, for her interest and assistance in the work which this book represents.

Warm thanks are also due to Mrs. George Hyman of Jasper, Florida, who took the time to escort us about Jasper, pointing out the former Smith residence, and to talk of her early friendship with the Smith family. Mr. George P. Brockway, President of W.W. Norton and Company, Inc., very generously loaned the company's file of correspondence with Lillian Smith to the authors for their perusal and use. Thanks are also due the librarians at The Robert Manning Strozier Library of Florida State University who were patiently helpful in the search for both primary and secondary reference materials.

LOUISE BLACKWELL

Florida A. & M. University

FRANCES CLAY

Florida State University

Acknowledgments

Grateful acknowledgment is made to the following for permission to use quotations:

Harcourt, Brace & World, Inc., for excerpts from Lillian Smith's *Strange Fruit* and *One Hour*.

W.W. Norton & Company, Inc., for excerpts from Lillian Smith's *Memory of a Large Christmas* and *Our Faces, Our Words*, and also *Killers of the Dream*, Copyright 1949, (C) 1961 by Lillian Smith.

The World Publishing Co. for excerpts from Lillian Smith's *The Journey*.

Miss Lillian Smith for excerpts from *Now Is the Time*.

Mrs. George Jean Nathan (Miss Julie Haydon) for excerpts from *The Theatre Book of the Year 1945-46* by George Jean Nathan.

University of Minnesota Press for excerpts from Stanley Edgar Hyman's *Flannery O'Connor*.

Contents

Chronology

1897   Lillian Smith born on December 12 in Jasper, Florida; daughter of Calvin Warren Smith and Anne (Simpson) Smith.

1911   Took a summer trip to Colorado.

1912   Family established a summer home at Clayton, Georgia.

1915   Graduated from high school in Jasper. Family moved permanent residence to Clayton, Georgia.

1915- Attended Piedmont College, Demorest, Georgia.
1916

1916- Helped father manage a winter hotel at Daytona Beach,
1917   Florida.

1917- Studied piano at Peabody Conservatory, Baltimore.
1918

1918- Returned to Clayton. Served as principal of a two-teacher
1919   school at Tiger, Georgia. Volunteered for Student Nurse Corps.

1919- Studied piano at Peabody Conservatory.
1922

1920- Worked with father during summer months, one summer as
1922   manager of a summer hotel and two summers as music counselor at Laurel Falls Camp for Girls.

1922- Served as head of music department at Virginia School,
1925   Huchow, Chekiang Province, China.

1925   Returned to Clayton as director of Laurel Falls Camp.

1925- Directed Laurel Falls Camp for Girls.
1949

1925- Spent two winters as secretary to brother, Austin, who was
1927   city manager of Fort Pierce, Florida.

1928- Studied at Teachers College, Columbia University.
1929

1930   Father died.

1930- Spent winters at Clayton and Macon, Georgia, drafting three
1935   manuscripts which were destroyed by fire in 1944: (1) a novel about China, entitled *And the Waters Flow On*, (2) a novel about the South, entitled *Tom Harris and Family*, and (3) a novella, *Every Branch in Me*.

1936 Edited and published, jointly with Paula Snelling, a little magazine, *Pseudopodia*.

1937 Traveled to Nova Scotia. Changed name of *Pseudopodia* to *The North Georgia Review*.

1938 Mother died. During winter months traveled to Brazil, where she worked on a novel, *Strange Fruit*.

1939 Received a Julius Rosenwald Fellowship for a travel-study project in the South.

1940 Received a second Julius Rosenwald Fellowship.

1942 Changed name of *The North Georgia Review* to *South Today*. "Burning Down Georgia's Back Porch," published in *Common Ground*.

1943 "Democracy Was Not a Candidate" and "Growing into Freedom" published in *Common Ground*.

1944 Published *Strange Fruit*. Made speech, "Freedom and Shame," under sponsorship of *Herald Tribune* Forum; "Humans in Bondage" published in *Social Action*; "Today's Children and Tomorrow's World," published in *Childhood Education*; "Southern Defensive" published in *Common Ground*; wrote letter to Blue Ridge Conference urging the integration of white and Negro YMCAs and YWCAs. Received the Constance Lindsay Skinner Award and the Page One Award. *Strange Fruit* banned in Boston. Fire destroyed her papers at Clayton.

1945 *Strange Fruit* dramatized by Lillian and Esther Smith; José Ferrer directed the play on Broadway. The novel, *Strange Fruit*, defended in court in Massachusetts. "Personal History of *Strange Fruit*," published in *Saturday Review of Literature*; "What Segregation Does to Our Children," in *Child Study*; "Growing Plays: The Girl," *Educational Leadership*; "How to Work for Racial Equality," *New Republic*; "Children Talking," *Progressive Education*; "Why I Wrote *Strange Fruit*," *Southern Literary Messenger*; "Addressed to White Liberals," in *Primer for White Folks*.

1946 Made trip to India as a member of the Famine Commission and guest of British government. *South Today* discontinued. Lived during fall and winter in Brooklyn Heights; worked on novel called *Julia*.

1947 Directed Laurel Falls Camp; traveled through western United States.

1948   Closed Laurel Falls Camp. Laid *Julia* aside; began writing *Killers of the Dream.*

1949   Published *Killers of the Dream.*

1950   Received honorary Doctor of Humane Letters degree from Howard University and honorary Doctor of Letters degree from Oberlin College; received National Book Award Committee's Special Citation for Distinguished Contribution to American Letters and Southern Authors' Award for *Killers of the Dream.*

1951   Gave speech on childhood in a biracial culture at Savannah, Georgia; gave speech "Ten Years from Today," at Kentucky State College (reprinted in *Vital Speeches*); "Walls of Segregation are Crumbling" published in *New York Times Magazine.* Began writing *The Journey.*

1952   Gave speech before the NAACP, Atlanta, Georgia, in protest of segregated schools; "Declaration of Faith in America" published in *New York Times Magazine.*

1953   Underwent surgery for cancer; completed *The Journey*; gave up apartment at Hotel Margaret in Brooklyn Heights.

1954   Published *The Journey.* Gave a Sidney Hillman Lecture at Roosevelt University on topic "Demagoguery: World-Size Danger. Have We World-Size Defenses?"

1954-   Spent six months in India, interviewing Prime Minister
1955   Nehru and other prominent figures for planned book; visited Rome, Paris, and London.

1955   Published *Now Is the Time.* Served as writer-in-residence at Vassar College; received Georgia Writers' Association Award for *The Journey.* Again fire destroyed her home and personal papers, including notes on India, at Clayton. "Prayer for a Better World" published in *Parents Magazine.*

1956   Rested for four months at Neptune Beach, Florida; published "Negroes in Gray Flannel Suits," an essay review of *How Far the Promised Land?* by Walter White, in *The Progressive.*

1957   Received honorary degree of Doctor of Humane Letters from Atlanta University; received the Franklin D. Roosevelt Citation awarded by Americans for Democratic Action. "No Easy Way, Now" published in the *New Republic.*

1958   "And Suddenly Something Happened" published in *Saturday Review.* Worked on *One Hour.*

1959   Published *One Hour.* Received the Freedom Award of the

Women's Committee of Roosevelt University.

1960   "Novelists Need a Commitment" published in *Saturday Review*.

1961   "Ordeal of Southern Women" published in *Redbook*. "Memory of a Large Christmas" published in *Life*.

1962   Published *Memory of a Large Christmas*; "Miss Smith of Georgia," a television documentary, produced by Time-Life Broadcasts; received Sidney Hillman Award for best magazine writing in 1961 and responded with a speech, "The Awakening of the Heart," later published in *Redbook*. "Now, the Lonely Decision for Right or for Wrong," in *Life*; "The Mob and the Ghost," in *Progressive*; "A Strange Kind of Love" and "No More Ladies in the Dark," in *Saturday Review*. Learned she had lung cancer.

1963   "Too Tame the Shrew" and "Thoughts as My Travels End" published in *Saturday Review*. Spent winter in Jacksonville, Florida; gave speech, "Women Born of Man," at Stetson University; lectured in Los Angeles.

1963-   Treated for cancer.
1964

1964   Returned to Clayton; published *Our Faces, Our Words*; received honorary degree of Doctor of Literature from Western Maryland College; "The Day It Happens to Each of Us" published in *McCall's*; "The Mob and the Ghost" reprinted in *Black, White and Gray*, edited by Bradford Daniel.

1965   Recorded *Our Faces, Our Words* for Spoken Arts. Received first Queen Esther Award from National Women's Division of American Jewish Congress and responded with a speech which was published in *Saturday Review* under title, "Poets Among the Demagogues."

1966   Received the Charles S. Johnson Award from Fisk University. Wrote letter to the editor of the *Atlanta Constitution* which was reprinted as "Miss Smith on SNCC" in *New South*. Died on September 28, in Atlanta, Georgia.

CHAPTER 1

Growth of a Legend

I *The Early Years*

FACT and fiction together made Lillian Eugenia Smith a legendary figure in her own lifetime. On the factual side, it can be said that Miss Smith, as long ago as 1936, identified herself with those persons, in the North and in the South, who wanted the South to change its racial patterns. On the fictional level, we find the idea, prevalent among her friends and enemies, that she was purely and simply a propagandist for racial integration. Miss Smith's image of herself was another matter entirely: she admitted to being a political liberal, but she saw herself as an artist who used her talent in the cause of mankind.

As her earliest writings indicate, Lillian Smith was keenly interested in the role of the artist in contemporary society.[1] Never a modest person, she was outspoken in her criticism of Southern politicians, of Western imperialism in China, of other writers, and of numerous groups and individuals with whom she did not agree. Her own candid language, in print and on the platform, served to obscure from public view some of her varied interests and talents.

The only way to determine who Lillian Smith was and what the legend has to do with truth is to trace as accurately as possible the significant facts in the life of this controversial Southern writer. She was born in Jasper, Florida, on December 12, 1897, where she lived until she graduated from high school in 1915. She was the seventh of nine children.[2] As she relates in *Killers of the Dream*, she had a comfortable and pleasant childhood:

> I was born and reared in a small Deep South town whose population was about equally Negro and white. There were nine of us who grew up freely in a rambling house of many rooms, surrounded by big lawn, back yard, gardens, fields, and barn. It was the kind of home that gathers memories like dust, a place filled with laughter and play and pain and hurt and ghosts and games. We were given such advantages

of schooling, music, and art as were available in the South, and our world was not limited to the South, for travel to far places seemed a natural thing to us, and usually one of the family was in a remote part of the earth.

We knew we were a respected and important family of this small town but beyond this we gave little thought to status. Our father made money in lumber and naval stores for the excitement of making and losing it—not for what money can buy nor the security which it sometimes gives.[3]

The home, with its gables and porches, is still in use, but long since occupied by new owners. Looking from the front door of the house, across a narrow paved road, a railroad, and another narrow paved road, one looks into the front door of the Methodist church. The church, its structure having undergone some repairs through the years, is the same one the Smiths attended two or three times each Sunday. Many old friends of the Smith family still live in Jasper, and some of them confess that they have never read *Strange Fruit*.

Since Jasper is the thinly disguised Maxwell, Georgia, of *Strange Fruit*, the visitor naturally looks for identifiable landmarks. A ride through the Negro section reveals familiar sights and sounds, two-story houses, swinging gates, and unpaved roads; but the houses which were new in Miss Smith's childhood are old now and dilapidated. On the edge of the Negro district, however, modernity has come to Jasper in the form of all-brick public-housing units, sitting on a grassy flatland in the glaring sun. Jasper public schools had made no move toward integration as of the 1965-66 school year. This town, like thousands of other small towns across the country, is less thriving and less progressive than it was fifty years ago. But it must be remembered that Lillian Smith moved away from Jasper in 1915.

Many factors can be traced as possible influences on the direction and impact of Miss Smith's life. Her admiring references to her maternal grandfather indicate a strong influence from him, particularly in the areas of intellectual and cultural independence. He was William Henry Simpson, a New Yorker, who was reared in wealth and educated to be a Jesuit priest. Simpson left the Church and migrated to Georgia, where he eventually married Caroline Peeples, a member of a prominent Georgia family, owners of a rice plantation in the tidewater area of the state.

Anne Simpson, daughter of the aristocratic Henry and Caroline Simpson, married Calvin Warren Smith, whose ancestors had come from North Carolina to homestead in Ware County, Georgia. Although the Smiths had owned slaves, they were not an aristocratic family by Georgia standards. The Smiths were diligent, sensible, and self-respecting farmers. Miss Smith remembers her father as having a keen mind and as being a curious, energetic, and cheerful man. Her mother, she recalls, was an introspective, imaginative person, with a deep and quiet but passionate nature.

Calvin Warren Smith, it seems, had a lifelong yearning to be a preacher; but Miss Smith always felt that he would have been a good college professor since he liked to talk and to discuss ideas and values. Nevertheless, he was a tough businessman who prospered in wholesale lumber and naval-stores enterprises in Jasper. He did business through offices in Jacksonville and Savannah, and he made extended trips to New York City. When Lillian was four years old, he bought timber rights in the Biloxi-Gulfport area of Mississippi and moved his family by train to Gulfport. After six months, however, the family moved back to Jasper.

About 1912, Mr. Smith bought some land at Clayton, in the north Georgia mountains, and there he established a summer home for the family. With the beginning of World War I, the decline in the foreign market for lumber and naval stores caused drastic decrease in the fortunes of C. W. Smith. In the summer of 1915 Mr. Smith moved the family's permanent residence to Clayton, where he operated a summer hotel and eventually founded Laurel Falls Camp for Girls on top of Old Screamer Mountain.

Although a shortage of money caused Lillian to enroll in nearby Piedmont College at Demorset, Georgia, rather than in some more distant and prestigious institution, fortune seems to have worked in her favor. The college, which was under the auspices of Congregationalists from New England, was quite small. At the time of her enrollment, Lillian Smith recalled, there were only thirty-five students in the college division of the school; but the preparatory school was much larger. Most of the professors were from the East, graduates of such colleges as Smith, Wellesley, Yale, and Harvard; and the instruction in some courses was on a more or less tutorial basis. For instance, there were two students in Lillian's mathematics class which was taught by Dean Rogers who later became president of the University of Georgia. There were three students in her Latin class, taught by a woman graduate of Smith College.

Wendell Brooks Phillips, who held a masters degree from Harvard, taught a comparatively large English class of twenty students. Since Mr. Phillips was bored by freshman English, he taught what amounted to a sophomore English course similar to one he had had at Harvard. Miss Smith recalled that she and two or three other students eagerly absorbed Mr. Phillips's comprehensive course in English literature from Beowulf to the twentieth century. He did not touch on contemporary writers, but the young Lillian had read them for herself, having started to read adult books at the age of ten.

In the Jasper home there had been a large family library, a shrine to her maternal grandfather; and, before entering Piedmont College, Lillian Smith had read all of Shakespeare's plays, all of Milton, Hawthorne, Dickens, and Tennyson. She had read the Bible through several times. Naturally she had also read many books of minor literary merit. In any event, she was reasonably well prepared for the advanced English class which Mr. Phillips conducted.

At the end of one year, Lillian Smith left college to help her parents with family businesses. She worked with her father in the mountains during the summer, and in the fall she went with him to Daytona Beach, Florida, where he leased and operated a hotel during the winter months (1916-17). During this time, she met and fell in love with a violinist from New York, a man twice her age. She was impressed by the fact that he had studied in Europe and with Joachim. Urged on by her musician friend, Miss Smith decided to pursue her own interest in a musical career, and she enrolled at Peabody Conservatory in Baltimore for the year 1917-18. She studied piano with Emanuel Wad from Denmark, who considered her to be a very talented musician.

The year in Baltimore was inspiring but difficult for the petite musician from the South. Her instructors praised her, and she was given extra piano lessons at the expense of the school. She had to work, however, to support herself; and she did so mainly by accompanying singers and by conducting gym and ballet classes at the YWCA. She lived at Margaret Bennett Home, an endowed home for needy students and working girls. In the summer of 1918, having broken with her musician friend, Miss Smith returned to Clayton where she joined the Student Nursing Corps. Since she was subject to call by the U. S. Army, she did not return to Baltimore in the fall.

After the Armistice, she was released from the corps; and, upon the urging of school officials and her father, she became a teacher-principal in a two-teacher mountain school a few miles from her home in Tiger, Georgia. In addition to her administrative duties, she taught the fifth, sixth, seventh, and eighth grades; the second teacher taught grades one through four. Although the school term lasted only four months, Miss Smith made the best of those rugged winter months in the mountains. From Sunday to Friday of each week she lived in the home of a mountain family. The toilet was out-of-doors, the washbasin was on the back porch, and the family cooked on an open fireplace. Living in general was frugal. For breakfast, there was usually poor coffee, hoecakes with fresh butter, and sometimes jelly. For lunch, there might be canned tomatoes, corn-meal hoecakes, buttermilk, and sometimes turnip greens. Supper consisted of hoecake, butter, home canned peaches, and a little fresh pork or home-cured salt-bacon. Each Friday afternoon, Lillian Smith walked three and a half miles across the mountains to her home.

When the other teacher in Lillian's school resigned, Lillian's younger sister, Esther, came to teach with Lillian. Together they instituted various creative activities such as school plays, games, singing, and Saturday night parties for families. As principal, it was Lillian's duty to visit various families in the school community, which she did, sometimes spending the night in their homes.

In the fall of 1919, Miss Smith returned to Baltimore and her studies at Peabody Conservatory, where she spent the next three school years. To support herself, she had to find new jobs in Baltimore. She recalls that she almost starved to death the first few months she was there before she could get enough jobs as an accompanist to meet her financial needs. Her work as accompanist and her practice kept her at the piano many long hours each day. Often she did not have five cents to ride the trolley and would walk home from Peabody, a distance of twenty-four blocks, sometimes through rain, sleet, or snow. She had little money for food and none for galoshes. She did not complain to her parents, however, because they would have insisted that she return home if they had known how difficult her situation was.

Miss Smith took on various paying jobs such as addressing envelopes at night for the Democratic party, playing for gymnasium classes in the recreation department of the American Can Company, and teaching music in a rough neighborhood near the waterfront. She also taught a Sunday School class for an Episcopal mission in the slums of Baltimore, where she learned about city poverty, factory life, and the general misery of city slums. Even so, she thought of herself as avant-grade, Bohemian, liberal, an artist for art's sake. She dated John Hopkins medical students and through all of her various activities made many lasting friends while in Baltimore.

Despite constant encouragement from her professors at Peabody, Lillian Smith began to realize that her type of creative playing was not the kind of talent required for the concert stage. Moreover, her hands were too small. At the end of four years of study, she accepted her limitations and decided to accept a position as head of the music department in Virginia School in Huchow, Chekiang Province of China—a mission school for middle-class and wealthy Chinese girls. Although Miss Smith was not a missionary, she was strongly identified with the mission work being done in China; for one of her sisters and her brother-in-law had gone to China as missionary-teachers as early as 1910. Lillian Smith went to China in 1922.

During the period that Miss Smith was in China, major changes were taking place in the social and political structure of the country. She was there when the Kuomintang declaration based upon the San Min doctrine was issued in 1924. Dr. Sun Yat-sen had first outlined the San Min doctrine, or the Three Principles of the People, in 1907. The first doctrine of the Kuomintang declaration had to do with nationalism, which had two aspects: (1) freedom of China from imperialistic domination and (2) racial equality for all people resident in China. The second doctrine called for both direct and indirect democracy, meaning that the people should have not only the right of suffrage but also the rights of initiative, referendum, and recall. And third was the doctrine of livelihood, which included two points: (1) the equalization of land ownership and (2) the regulation of capital. Miss Smith recalled that she was aware of and disturbed by colonialism and its effects on China. And she also recalled the fierce struggles among the warlords for power. Her thinking on racial equality must have been strongly affected by the interracial problems which she observed in China.

In 1925 she returned to Georgia where she again observed the poor and subservient Negro people and to the north Georgia mountains where she again encountered the problems of the poor white people. During the next five years she worked with her father in Clayton, with her brother in Florida, and studied for one school year at Teachers College, Columbia University. In 1930 her father died, leaving her with heavy family responsibilities which she did not hesitate to assume.

With regard to her lifelong responses to the needs of her family, Miss Smith described herself as having two sides to her nature. Her "Martha" side she defined as her need to be practical, to help her family through difficult periods, to do her duty. But she had a "Mary" side which called her back from noncreative chores to do creative things. The two needs which she had—the need to perform her duty as she saw it and the need to be creative—probably account for the fact that the bulk of her writings reflect her actual experiences in life. As any aspiring artist knows, a strong conscience in favor of doing one's duty can be destructive of creative talent. For this reason, Lillian Smith was grateful for her "Mary" side which insisted that she reserve a part of her life for creative work.

In spite of heavy responsibilities as director of Laurel Falls Camp and in caring for her invalid mother, the six or seven years following the death of her father were fruitful years for her development as a writer. She found time to draft a novel on China, a novel about a Southern family which she called *Tom Harris and Family*, and a novella. All of these manuscripts and numerous other valuable items were destroyed by a fire in her study in 1944.

Her career as a published author actually began in the spring of 1936 when she and her good friend, Paula Snelling, founded a little magazine. In the following thirty years, Miss Smith was an editor, novelist, playwright; and she wrote nonfiction books, articles, critical essays, and newspaper columns; and this book is concerned primarily with these writings. An attempt has been made to identify and discuss, in this brief volume, the significant writings of Miss Smith's long and active career.

II *The Mature Years*

During her thirty years as a public figure, Lillian Smith suffered her share of losses and disappointments; but she also enjoyed fame, fortune, and high honor. Although she was never to visit China again, she traveled extensively in her own country and abroad.

After the death of her mother in 1938, she and Miss Snelling took a freighter trip to Brazil where they spent several months in the town of Belem.

In 1939 and 1940 she received Rosenwald fellowships for travel and study in the Southern United States. Although she had become well known through her writings in the magazine which she helped to establish, she became widely famous and earned a great deal of money with the publication of her first novel, *Strange Fruit*, in 1944. That same year, while she was in New York, her secretary and some of her friends were in her study at Clayton when a faulty heater flue caused the building to burn. The loss of Miss Smith's manuscripts, Chinese memorabilia, and other personal papers was irreparable.

In 1946, Miss Smith was appointed to the Famine Commission and visited India as a guest of the British government. She was to visit India again, with Miss Snelling as companion, in 1954-55, when she had a series of interviews with Prime Minister Nehru and other prominent officials. She made notes for a book about Nehru, but later on in 1955 her home in Clayton was deliberately burned by two white youths. Thus once again her accumulated papers, manuscripts, and notes—this time on India—were destroyed.

In 1948 Miss Smith closed Laurel Falls Camp for Girls and afterward devoted herself wholly to her literary career. On June 9, 1950, she received her first honorary degree, a Doctor of Humane Letters, from Howard University. The citation, in the form of an indictment, was witty but serious. It read in part as follows:

Lillian Smith you are a revolutionist. You go about this country speaking and writing words which have no other purpose but to destroy and to displace habits of life, institutional pathways, though patterns and emotions which we people of the South and in the colonial possessions all over the world have followed with what we have considered to be indispensable devotion for nearly 300 years.

You are a dangerous revolutionist. There is enough dynamite in what you say to blow up the very foundation of segregated civilization.

A few days later, on June 12, she received a Doctor of Letters degree from Oberlin College, the citation read in part as follows:

Had Miss Lillian Smith been born and reared almost any place north of the Mason-Dixon line, her books on race problems might have been accepted without causing much flurry in the literary and sociological worlds. Had her ancestors been members of the Wellington rescue party or graduates of Oberlin College, we might have expected this conscience—which evidently impels her to write books on the race question—as part of her heritage.

Only those of us who lived in the south know what a hard and tough way of life she has selected for herself in deliberately choosing to make herself the forceful, articulate and vehement spokesman for a new southern reformist movement.

When, in 1957, Atlanta University awarded Miss Smith an honorary Doctor of Humane Letters degree, the citation called her an "ardent lover of the South, who senses its weakness and its strength." Then in 1964 Western Maryland College awarded her an honorary Doctor of Literature degree. The citation read: "Motivated in no way by political opportunism or selfish interest, but rather by a deep, philosophical purpose and conviction of right, this daughter of the south who knows and loves the south, through novel and essay, by personal living and eloquent word, has given articulate expression and sympathetic challenge in behalf of the God-given dignity and freedom of each human personality."

This last degree was awarded to Miss Smith in absentia because she was too ill with cancer to attend the ceremonies. Although she suffered recurrent cancer after 1953, she continued to write and to make public appearances until shortly before her death. Twice she was honored in the South for her writings: in 1950 she was awarded the Southern Authors' Award for *Killers of the Dream*, and in 1955 she received the Georgia Writers' Association Award for *The Journey*. Also, in 1950 she received the National Book Award Committee's Special Citation for Distinguished Contribution to American Letters.

In her final years, Miss Smith lived in a pleasant mountaintop cottage at Clayton. Always an omnivorous reader, she continued to delve deeply into psychology, sociology, theology, philosophy, fiction, and poetry. Although she had to make periodic trips for treatment to the Emory University Cancer Center in Atlanta, her spirits remained high and she worked on several books, including a collection of essays. A legend in her own lifetime, she remained a busy and alert figure to the last. One of her last public acts was her resignation from the Congress of Racial Equality (CORE) because its leaders seemed to abandon the nonviolent approach to racial problems in accepting the Black Power ideas of Stokely Carmichael. She died September 28, 1966, at Emory University Hospital in Atlanta.

CHAPTER 2

The Editor

I *Birth of a Magazine*

T HE founding of a little magazine frequently grows out of the desire of one or two people to have an outlet for their own ideas and to have a place where they can publish their own works. There must also be, in the thinking of the founders, a conviction that there are some other people around the country who would like to read the kind of magazine that is to be published. These premises obviously were involved during that long, cold, idle winter of 1935-36 when Paula Snelling and Lillian Smith conceived and developed the idea of publishing a little magazine with the unlikely title of *Pseudopodia;* the first issue of the quarterly, containing twelve unnumbered pages, appeared in the spring of 1936. The editorial page listed Paula Snelling, editor, and Lillian E. Smith, associate editor. An unsigned editorial in the first issue read in part as follows:

The name *Pseudopodia* was chosen partly as outlet for the last vestige of our sophomoric impulses; partly to give encouragement to certain of those whose attempts at artistic expression have met with obstacles and rebuffs. For the artist no less than the amoeba inhabits an adamant world in which cherished efforts at locomotion fail not always through inner incapacity. A pseudopod differs from an ordinary foot in that it is not a specialized and differentiated organ fully equipped with toenails and callouses but a temporary and tender projection of the nucleus or inner-self, upon the success of whose gropings the nucleus is entirely dependent for its progress and sustenance. We believe that there are artists, some acclaimed, others groaning so to be, who have put much of themselves into writings which you and we would enjoy but for one reason or another have not appeared in the big magazines. We want to read and publish some of those manuscripts.

Since *Pseudopodia* is too small to roam the world it will concern itself mainly with the south. Specifically, with whatever seems to us artistic, vital, significant which is being done by writers who have their cultural roots here whatever their present locale and interest may be, and by those from no matter where who have been grafted to us, and are now bearing fruit nourished by our soil.

We are not interested in perpetuating that sterile fetishism of the Old South which has so long gripped our section. We believe that the saline state which befell Lot's wife did not come by divine whim. That petrification follows inevitably from looking too exclusively at the past; at past glories no less than at past orgies. Time, abetted by *Wrigley's*, moves too inexorably on for any living Joshua or Jurgen to stay it.

It is our wish to encourage and where we are able to help the development of whatever seems to us good among the young artists and aspirants of today. But in the many places where we think we see vapidness, dishonesty, cruelty, stupidity, we wish to expose rather than gloss over. After our right eye has offended our neighbors of the north and they have self-righteously plucked it out for us the need becomes acute for devising less devastating means for treating the ailment in our left.

We hope that those southerners who have already achieved national recognition will be interested enough to contribute here. And that those less fortunate who know the loneliness and discouragement of the different at the mercy of demons will turn here for possible recognition and stimulation.

We can pay no money. Each June we do invite our contributors of the year to spend a few days at our mountain home, Laurel Falls, where they may swim, play tennis, sleep, talk—or write. And there is an annual prize of $5.00 each for the best poem and the best piece of prose submitted.[1]

Although the composition of that first editorial was a joint effort of the editors, certain stylistic aspects point to the writing of Lillian Smith. Her tendency throughout the years to write fragmentary sentences is evident in paragraphs two and three of the above passage. Also, her persistent tendency to begin sentences with conjunctions is evident in this early writing. Her unorthodox use of the semicolon can be seen in her writings of thirty years later as well as in this first editorial.

While the editorial referred to the needs of artists for publishing outlets, it also invited social and political criticism of the South. At any rate, the mixed goals of the editorial were prophetic of the future career of Lillian Smith who continued to divide her time and energies between the writing of fiction and the espousal of social and political causes.

From the first issue through the ten-year life of the magazine, Miss Smith published a column entitled "Dope with Lime." Under that heading, she used her column to expound on whatever subject tempted her at the moment, including tantalizing suggestions as to what would appear in the following issue. In her first column, she promised that the next issue of *Pseudopodia* would carry a review of *Who Owns America*, edited by Herbert Agar and Allen Tate. Miss Smith wrote: "Pehaps most of us remember Mr. Tate best for his contribution to *I'll Take My Stand* which some of us thought brilliantly untenable.²

Thus from the very first issue, the editors set themselves up in opposition to the Nashville Fugitive-Agrarian group. The promised review, entitled "Southern Agrarianism: Revised Version" by John D. Allen, was the featured essay in the second issue of the magazine. Mr. Allen's views apparently coincided with those of the editors, and he closed his essay with the following sentences: "It is a pity that a program so futile, a social philosophy so warped and partial, can be urged with a charm and vigor so dangerously seductive. It is regrettable that with their recent attention to economics, they have studiously shunned the unorthodox. It is lamentable, but it is true, that the Fugitives are still in flight."³

In the third issue of the magazine, Lillian E. Smith wrote a review of Margaret Mitchell's *Gone with the Wind* under the title "One More Sigh for the Good Old South."⁴ While revealing herself to be an unsure critic, she helped to clarify the stance she and her magazine would take in book reviews of the future. She set out to condemn *Gone with the Wind*, but she condemned and praised it for the wrong reasons. Obviously, she had been reading the group of American critics known as the Naturalistic-Sociological-Marxist school, some of the leaders of which were V. F. Calverton, Michael Gold, and Granville Hicks. She was also imbued with the psychological-psychoanalytical approach to criticism. As can be seen, she mixed the two approaches in her criticism of *Gone with the Wind*. The following passage from the review illustrates the influence of the radical group of critics:

An artist comprehends the social-economic-intellectual assumptions of a period, their implications and effect upon personality but surely he must remain detached and critical of them. Just as it would be difficult for most of us today when half the world is starving or killing or preparing to kill each other and many of the other half tangled up despairingly in their own emotional problems, to take seriously the feuds, conventions, snobbery and ambitions of Atlanta's Society Set (or any other town's) so it is difficult for us to read without boredom of the trivial social snobbery of the Atlanta of Reconstruction Days.[5]

Miss Smith's point, as the world now knows, was lost on the American reading public. Still, her reference to the *artist* is significant because she always thought of herself as an artist and because she remained, throughout the years, fairly certain in her own mind as to what the artist is and what he ought to do. In the case of *Gone with the Wind*, her allusion to the *artist* was irrelevant primarily because Margaret Mitchell did not think of herself as one. Miss Mitchell, a newspaper woman, simply wrote a historical romance of the South; but, even if she had considered herself a serious writer of fiction, she might well have claimed the writer's prerogative to choose her material and to present it as best she could.

In the same review, Miss Smith made a conscious effort to dissociate herself from the Marxist critics by the following statement: "As we protest the interpretation of our American life today solely in terms of Capitalistic (or of Marxist) ideology so we protest the interpretation, however unconscious, of Southern life seventy years ago in nostalgic terms of old Planter-ideology."[6] But, at the same time that she was protesting the author's interpretation, Miss Smith rendered Miss Mitchell the following widow's mite: "Her knowledge of the Civil War-Reconstruction period is admirable and so precise and comprehensive is her acquaintance with the customs of the time and the scenes of that early, young Atlanta that she achieves an atmosphere of contemporaneity (despite hoop skirts and stays) which is the nature of a *tour de force*."[7]

Finally, Miss Smith used the psychological-psychoanalytical ax on Miss Mitchell and her book: "To attempt the creation of character, the probing of personality without recognizing and comprehending the dynamic force of the unconscious as it plays upon and determines so powerfully the external manifestations of personality is, frankly, to be naive. Whether we wish it or no, the findings of Freud and his followers have not only made for us enormous extensions of knowledge in the realms of the spirit but by their very nature are changing the intrinsic quality of that spirit."[8]

The New Criticism was increasing its influence rapidly in 1936-37, but Lillian Smith, writing in *Pseudopodia*, gave evidence that she had little interest in it or its exponents in the South. She continued in her critical writing through the years to mix her own brand of "social-economic-intellectual assumptions" with Freudian psychology. She insisted upon the artist's having an over-all purpose other than the execution of the immediate work. As recently as 1960 she wrote an article entitled "Novelists Need a Commitment,"[9] and in 1965 she criticized Flannery O'Connor for her lack of a sociological commitment.[10] On the other hand, in 1966 Miss Smith was quoted as saying: "I have never been a 'cause' person. I am concerned with the excellence of the human race—not white, black or yellow."[11]

The featured article and, in retrospect, the outstanding item in the third issue of the magazine was W. J. Cash's "The Reign of the Commonplace," which was later a part of his book, *The Mind of the South*. Cash's article opens with the following paragraph: "The final great result of Reconstruction we have to consider in this chapter (a result which stands as a sort of summation of the things we have been seeing) is that it established what I have called the savage ideal as it had not been established in any Western people since the decay of medieval feudalism, and almost as truly as it is established today in Fascist Italy, in Nazi Germany, in Soviet Russia—and so paralyzed Southern culture at the root."[12]

In the remainder of the essay, Cash discussed how Southerners, under the pressure of the Reconstruction, began to fuse their old ideas and loyalties and to make a sharp distinction between what was Southern and what was not: "In a word, here, explicitly defined in every great essential, defined in feeling down to the last detail, was what one must think and say and do." Those who didn't follow the Southern way had to be punished, either by the Ku Klux Klan or by the coercion of his neighbors. Cash also cited the damage done to North-South relationships by the "Yankee schoolma'am" who came south in large numbers to educate the Negro people and by the "peripatetic Yankee journalist" who also came in droves. Religious tolerance almost disappeared in the South, and Cash placed a large part of the responsibility for this on Southern Protestant ministers. The ministers, he contended, equated Northern thinking with such modern thinkers as Darwin and Huxley; and they set about molding the minds of their church members accordingly.

II *Growth of a Magazine*

In the second issue of *Pseudopodia*, the editorial page listed Paula Snelling and Lillian E. Smith as editors, the title of associate editor having been dropped. This issue, which had grown to sixteen pages, contained "Hymn to the Cicada," by Wendell Brooks Phillips, Miss Smith's freshman English teacher. There were frequent attempts at satire, in the early issues of the magazine, on the South and on such writers as Erskine Caldwell and William Faulkner. Miss Smith's opinion of Faulkner, as expressed at various times, was that he had a great deal of imagination but no brains.

One item published was a so-called drama-poem, "Well Hel-lo!" by Margery De Leon. The piece is neither drama nor poem, and what the author's intention was is not clear. The work is a dialogue between two Southern young people, former sweethearts, who are shy and not very expressive. The most that can be said for it is that it is an incidental dialogue which does not come off. It is not satirical, it is not humorous, and it cannot be taken seriously—which leads up to the fact that we look in vain for humor in the magazine and in the works of Lillian Smith.

One unsigned editorial, which can be attributed because of its stylistic characteristics to Miss Smith, indulges her sociological interest. The title of the editorial, which reads in part as follows, is "From Lack of Understanding": "But in addition to this need for understanding our state of mind—and of course the very phrase 'The South' is a state of mind—we need detailed and comprehensive facts concerning our immediate, multiple-faceted and paradoxical dilemma interpreted against historical backgrounds. And this Howard W. Odum gives us in an admirable way in *Southern Regions of the United States* (to be reviewed in our next issue)—a full-size picture of our potentialities and our deficiencies, buttressed up by 700 indices and 600 maps and charts."[13]

As this passage shows, Miss Smith had already developed a breathless style, a style which reminds the reader of a talker who is afraid he will be interrupted before he finishes what he has to say. She was and continued to be fond of beginning sentences with conjunctions. The third paragraph of this editorial is actually one sentence of some 450 words, despite the fact that some sections of it trail off with three dots (. . .) followed by a capital letter. Why Miss Smith remained so devoted to this device in her own work when there is no question of ellipsis is not clear.

Issue No. 4 of *Pseudopodia,* which had twenty pages, contained a review of a first novel, *Stubborn Roots,* by Elma Godchaux, in which Miss Smith revealed again her psychological approach to criticism. The following passage suffices:

We who have worked with the neurotic and psychotic know they do and feel much as we do and feel, only to a more painful or ecstatic or logical degree; have much the same impulses less carefully restrained; are as human as those of us who have the illusion that we are normal; and it is quite possible and easy to identify ourselves sympathetically with them. The old "there but for the grace of God . . ." seems to this reviewer not only relevant to actual life but an artistic necessity in character creation, howsoever strange or pathological or "normal" the character may be.[14]

In the spring of 1937, the editors changed the name of their magazine to *The North Georgia Review,* issuing Volume II, No. 1. The magazine had grown to twenty-four pages, but its format remained much the same. Miss Smith reviewed a novel by a Negro author, *A Long Way from Home* by Claude McKay, and a biography of a Negro poet, *Paul Laurence Dunbar* by Benjamin Brawley. Later Miss Smith said that during this time she was reading everything she could find by or about Negroes, and it was natural that the number of books reviewed on the subject of the Negro increased during the next few years.

The summer issue, 1937, carried an essay with which the editors obviously did not agree, "Apologia of a Dictator" by Morrison Calladay. This article was an attempt by Mr. Calladay to show the workings of Huey Long's mind and to present a case for fascism. Glenn W. Rainey, who had previously published poetry in the magazine, answered Callaway in an article entitled "A Brief for Freedom."

With the appearance of the winter 1937-38 issue, which had grown to thirty-two pages, Lillian E. Smith's name was listed above Paula Snelling's on the editorial page. An outstanding feature of this issue was the publication of Lillian Smith's first essay on China. It appeared as an editorial, "He That Is Without Sin,"[15] and ran to some four thousand words. Developed in the form of a dialogue between the author and an unknown friend in China, the editorial amounts to a reminiscence of how China got the way it was at the time of Miss Smith's sojourn there. The dialogue takes place on a

Saturday afternoon, May 30, 1925, with the author and her conversationalist sitting in a boat in a canal in Chekiang Province. The other woman explains to Miss Smith that hostility between the Chinese and the British began in 1839 with the Opium War, that in 1895 the Japanese succeeded in taking Korea away from China, that Britain continued to take over port cities, that Germany seized Tsingtao in 1897, which gave Russia an excuse to occupy Port Arthur. The Russian seizure in turn led France to claim Kwangchow-wa. When Miss Smith asks, "And the United States?" her friend replies: "Uncle Sam was busy with other matters, Hawaii and the Philippiness, but called to the boys to be sure to keep the door open."

As mentioned previously, Lillian Smith felt very strongly about imperialism in China; and her purpose in the present essay was to present the evils of the system and the damages done to the Chinese people as she saw them. The dialogue is laced with some fine descriptive passages such as the following: "A small houseboat with five ragged, dirty, redcheeked children on its deck, and a pot of pink geranium, drew up close, suddenly darted out into the stream. The train of boats circled a small island on which stood an old crumbling pagoda. A junk with red-brown sail bellied out by the breeze glided by. The stream grew narrow again. On either side were dull blobs of graves, here and there the yellow of a fresh coffin.[16]

As her title indicated, Miss Smith saw all of the major powers as sinners in their treatment of China. She made her point extremely well in the semifictional treatment of the first three-fourths of the piece, but the mood was disturbed and the impact weakened by three paragraphs of moralizing at the end. As the following diatribe indicates, she dissipated the finely built-in moral of her dialogue:

And now tonight, January, 1938, as I write, the pictures of the Panay incident are being shown throughout the country and once more anger and hate and prejudices are being fanned into flames. To what end? This time it is against the Japanese. Three men were killed in the Panay incident, ruthlessly, without excuse. But remember, twelve years ago six Chinese youngsters were killed by the British, as ruthlessly, as needlessly. "The Japanese have no right in China; we can't sit by and see them steal her wealth and kill her people!" You hear it every day. But we Western imperialists have been stealing her wealth and killing her people for 100 years. "We can't sit by . . . there's our national honour

. . ." No? We sit by and let our neighbors' children starve and do nothing about it. We sit by and see Negroes lynched and make no effort to punish the mob. We are not outraged when textile workers are killed, when miners starve. We've closed our eyes to the depredations Great Britain has made upon India; Gandhi has been for most of us only a stooge for our wisecracks. We forget Africa; we forget Mexico; the Philippines.[17]

The final paragraph, a hysterical summation of the situation of the United States as World War II was building up, contains references to Franklin Roosevelt and Alfred Landon and to Woodrow Wilson's war to "Make the world safe for democracy."

The next China material which Miss Smith published appeared in the summer issue of 1938. Under the title "And the Waters Flow On,"[18] she published some vignettes of China, its people, and its missionaries. Reading these passages makes us regret that Miss Smith's manuscript about China was destroyed by fire:

Across the city in an inner apartment of a wealthy silk merchant's home sat his wife and little wife gambling at mah jong. Fat, sleek, crafty, with black hair smoothly drawn back from their faces, they sat across from each other gossiping amiably and smoking cigarette after cigarette. They had been thus since late afternoon. Near each sat an old amah fanning her mistress—for the evening was warm and they had eaten heavily at a birthday feast at noon. Two bowls of tea now grown cold were nearby. The old amahs sleepily watched the moves made by their mistresses as they tirelessly played on and on.

. . . . . .

Under the matting roof of a small boat wedged in among hundreds of others on the canal at West Gate, a small child whimpered restlessly. The mother sleepily felt around in the dark, found the crying child from among five sleeping ones at her feet, picked it up, gave it her breast, patted the shoulder of another near her head who had stirred—and again fell asleep.[19]

The third and fourth issues of Volume III were published together with Lillian E. Smith writing an editorial of some two thousand words under the title, "Wanted: Lessons in Hate."[20] The word "hate" had appeared in her first essay on China, and with the present editorial it began to appear more and more frequently in her writings. "Wanted: Lessons in Hate" obviously grew out of her interest in psychology and her convictions as to what the artist could and ought to do. Her thesis is that man needs some kind of pagan demonology through which to vent his hatred and thus avoid venting it on other men. The following quotation summarizes her point: "We have never so needed these poets, artists, and preachers as we need them today to set up in vivid, concrete immediate terms a new demonology made up of the real enemies of mankind and to so kindle man's imagination that his hate will be turned against them instead of against himself."[21]

The editorial is a sermon which became uncontrolled. Since the word "hate" is one of the strongest words in the English language, it should be used sparingly, but Miss Smith seemed to be unable to avoid it. She apparently struggled with the word and its meaning for some years, for she was quoted in April, 1966 as saying: "An artist should remember that he cannot have hate in his nature. He has to have compassion. Everybody sins; everybody is evil, and everybody can be good."[22]

With Volume VII, the *North Georgia Review* became *South Today*. In an editorial entitled "Are We Not All Confused?," Miss Smith affirmed the belief of the editors that the welfare, happiness, and security of the Negro are as essential to them and to society as they are for the white man. And she chided almost everybody for neglect of the Negro: "We white liberals cannot in honesty blame the demagogues for stirring up race trouble; nor can we in decency accuse Negro leaders of exploiting the war emergency. We do our full share of both by our faintheartedness, our covering up of actual conditions, our personal snobbery, our selfish habit of putting private affairs, state politics, business interests and desire to be 'gentlemen' ahead of deep fundamental human needs."[23]

Later that year, Miss Smith wrote a long article in which she said that "perhaps the psychology of no group of people shows heavier traces of guilt and fear and hate than that of our South." She thought that the region's concern with religion made it impossible for its residents to treat the Negro inhumanely without suffering guilt. And "The improverished whites feel it more crudely as a vague mass-guilt" which makes them doubt their own capacity for doing good. The poor white, according to her theory, utilizes all of his energy in *"not doing harm."*

From time to time, Lillian Smith returned to the subject of faulty sex training of little children. In one "Dope with Lime" column she discussed the cultural situation which denies to little boys the opportunity to play with dolls or to play at life and love with out guilt feelings. She regretted the fact that American males who have an interest in cooking, health care, or babies are considered effeminate. With her psychoanalytic approach to child rearing, she naturally felt that every tolerance should be shown little children in their growth toward satisfactory sexual adjustment.

Although the magazine was continued for several issues after the publication of her novel *Strange Fruit* in 1944, the magazine had served its purpose. Through editorials, columns, articles, and excerpts from her novels, Lillian Smith had laid out the direction of her future writing. With the publication of *Strange Fruit*, various public forums and publishing outlets were immediately available to her. Through her own magazine, she had attained wide recognition as a Southern liberal and as a Southern white woman who dared to oppose segregation and to discuss Freudian psychology in public print. Her novel made her, overnight, a national figure.

CHAPTER 3

Of Fame and Fortune: **Strange Fruit**

I N February, 1944, Lillian Smith's first novel, *Strange Fruit*, was published by Reynal and Hitchcock. The work, which had been turned down by seven or eight publishers, was submitted under the title *Jordan Is So Chilly*. A change in title was suggested by the publishers; and Miss Smith, after careful thought, decided upon two words she had used in previous writings in which she had described Southern white culture as the "strange fruit" of racism. She and the publishers were pleased with the new title.

On March 19, 1944, *Strange Fruit* was declared obscene and removed from sale in Boston. *Publishers Weekly*, on the following April 15, showed *Strange Fruit* in fifth place on its list of best sellers. On May 15, the United States Post Office banned *Strange Fruit* from the mails; but this ban was lifted within a few hours because, according to Miss Smith, Mrs. Eleanor Roosevelt talked to President Roosevelt, and an order to revoke the ban was issued from the White House. The book was banned by "gentlemen's agreement" in Detroit in mid-May when a police sergeant visited booksellers and suggested that they not sell the book.

The sergeant's method worked until he reached the United Automobile Workers' Book Shop where the manager refused to follow his suggestion. The manager of the bookshop said that, as long as the book was available in the Detroit Public Library, it would be available in his shop. Immediately the United Automobile Workers' executives instructed the union attorneys to prepare to defend the bookshop if legal action were instigated by the police department. The Detroit Public Library, however, succeeded in preventing the official banning of *Strange Fruit* in Detroit; and the United Automobile Workers' Book Shop did not have to go to court. [1]

In the meantime, about April 1, 1944, Harold Williams, a Boston attorney, had made a public statement to the effect that someone should make a test case of the banning of *Strange Fruit* by the Boston Police Department. As a consequence, on April 4 Bernard DeVoto arranged to buy a copy of the book from Abraham Isenstadt in the presence of two policemen. DeVoto was subsequently found "not guilty" of violating the ban, but Isenstadt was found "guilty" and fined one hundred dollars. Upon appeal, the Massachusetts Supreme Judicial Court upheld Isenstadt's conviction on September 17, 1945. Because the publishers decided not to appeal to the United States Supreme Court, the ban on *Strange Fruit* has not as yet been lifted in Boston.[2]

Some of the furor over the novel, both in the North and in the South, stemmed from the fact that a Southern white woman was willing to oppose racial segregation by writing an exposé of segregation's lurid and inhumane aspects in the form of a novel. The theme of miscegenation aroused the ire of all kinds of people in the South; but in the North the theme was not objectionable—only the author's choice of words to develop her theme.

Although fame and fortune came suddenly to Lillian Smith, the novel which brought her notoriety was the outgrowth of long years of study and writing. She was actually working on *Strange Fruit* in 1938 when she traveled to Brazil. During the period between the inception of the work and its completion, Miss Smith traveled extensively through several Southern states in connection with the Rosenwald grants. She was, therefore, thoroughly familiar with her region; and her accuracy in depicting realistic details is evidence of her close observation. The novel is a Realistic-Naturalistic portrayal of life in a small Southern town in the 1920's. The fictional town, Maxwell, Georgia, bears some resemblance to Miss Smith's childhood hometown, Jasper, Florida. In her creation of characters, Miss Smith drew heavily upon her knowledge of psychology as well as upon her penchant for Realistic physical death.

I *The Narrative*

Briefly, *Strange Fruit* is, on the narrative level, the story of a secret love affair between Tracy Deen, a young white man who walks with a limp and who is the son of the town's doctor, and Nonnie Anderson, a pretty Negro college graduate, who has returned to Maxwell to work in domestic service for Mrs. Brown. Neither Tracy Deen nor Nonnie Anderson ever expected that they would marry each other, and there is no evidence that they ever discussed where or how their relationship would end. Throughout the years of the furtive relationship, Tracy meets the social demands of the white community by going out occasionally with Dorothy Pusey, who lives across the street. It is generally expected that Tracy and Dorothy will eventually marry each other.

The action of the novel is accelerated when Tracy, surrendering to pressure from his mother, decides to marry Dorothy. A person of weak motivation and a product of a materialistic society, he accepts the suggestion of a revivalist preacher, Brother Dunwoodie, that he give money to Nonnie and then pay someone to marry her. Tracy asks his Negro servant and friend, Henry McIntosh, to marry Nonnie, who is now pregnant. Accepting the notion that money can settle his problems, Tracy obtains money from his mother to pay Henry and to compensate Nonnie. Nonnie's brother, Ed, who is home on vacation from his job in Washington, D.C., senses that all is not well with Nonnie, although she has never confided in her family regarding Tracy.

When Henry McIntosh, out splurging with the money Tracy has given him, reveals that he has been paid to marry Nonnie, Ed Anderson overhears him. After delivering a few blows to Henry's face, Ed goes to waylay Tracy Deen, who is delivering her share of money to Nonnie. In the dark, Ed shoots and kills Tracy, leaving the body on the path from "colored town." With the money, untouched by Nonnie, that Tracy left lying on the fence rail, the Andersons help Ed to leave town during the night. A few hours later, Henry and his girl, Dessie, who have gone into the woods for sexual purposes, stumble upon Tracy's body. Henry, fearing that he will be charged with the murder, is unwilling to do more than pull the body off the path and hide it in the bushes. After the body is discovered, the white community seeks revenge in the form of a lynching—and innocent Henry McIntosh is the victim.

While there is no evidence that Miss Smith got the idea for her plot in *Strange Fruit* from an actual occurrence in Jasper, Florida, the history of the region is permeated with similar situations involving white men and black women and the lynching of Negro men. Neither is there any evidence that the characterization of Nonnie is based upon an actual person. Not anticipated by Miss Smith was the feeling generated against the book, and later the play, among Negro women graduates of Spelman College who said, and they continued to say as late as 1966, that "no Spelman girl" would do what Nonnie did. The most likely explanation is that Spelman College in Atlanta, a reputable college for Negro women, came readily to mind and that Miss Smith used it to emphasize the high quality of Nonnie's education, which was superior to that of most of the residents of Maxwell.

In speculating upon the source of Miss Smith's material and her reasons for writing *Strange Fruit*, it is safer to assume that she had a moral purpose in writing the novel and that she developed her plot, as most authors do, from the materials of history, experience, and imagination. For large numbers of readers the novel was concerned, on a significant level, with the stratification of society in a segregated Southern town. Given this level of interpretation and the author's moral purpose, then the reader must assume that Miss Smith deliberately wrote to shock the white South into seeing itself as she saw it.

II   *Social Determinism and Presentation*

With its dominant theme of social determinism, *Strange Fruit* fits solidly into the Naturalistic tradition; and, when judged by the standards of this tradition, it is a good and significant novel. The structure of the racially segregated society in Maxwell determines the behavior of both white and black citizens. This society determines that Nonnie Anderson, an attractive, college-educated Negro woman, must work as a domestic servant, or not work at all, because more appropriate positions are not open to her in Maxwell. Society will not tolerate an open courtship between whites and blacks, and thus Tracy and Nonnie must be furtive and dishonest about their love. Society is responsible for the hypocritical religious attitudes of white people in Maxwell since custom requires that the individual attend one of the accepted Protestant churches or be ostracized. In the context of this novel, the social structure is responsible for the inhibited and consequently unhealthy development of attitudes toward sex and child-rearing of white women; and Mrs. Deen, who is discussed later in this chapter, is an example.

Strange Fruit's overriding theme of social determinism spawns two other significant themes, violence and taboo, which strengthen the novel's place in the Naturalistic tradition. Because of the tensions generated in a society structured on racial segregation, violence is a natural consequence when behavior deviates from the expected pattern. In this novel, obvious tensions exist between the need of the black people for personal freedom and the determination of white people to see that black people "stay in their places," between the desire of Negroes to protect themselves and the denial of their legal processes by whites, between the Negro's struggle for survival and the white employer's exploitation of him, between the poor whites who fear the loss of jobs to Negroes and the Negroes who must work to survive, and between the whites who harbor fears regarding sex and violence on the part of the Negro and the Negroes who must bear the brunt of these fears.

It is no surprise, then, given the tensions which lie near the surface in Maxwell's society, that Ed Anderson should take violent steps to defend his sister; in such an environment, no other course of action is open to him. He cannot go to court to seek a settlement for his pregnant sister. Neither the law nor social mores will permit marriage, nor even admission that a love affair exists. On the other hand, after Tracy is killed, the social structure requires reprisal. The question of justice for the killer is barely considered in the white community, for the dominant race concedes no right or privileges to the minority race.

It was, of course, Miss Smith's bold approach in dealing with taboos—including the crude sexual obsessions of white people, miscegenation, and the failure of Christianity—that resulted in the banning of *Strange Fruit* in Boston and in assults upon the book in other cities. In Northern cities, objections were raised against the language describing sex and the human body. For instance, the Boston Police Department found "pointed breasts" objectionable. In the South, where no attempt was made to ban *Strange Fruit*, criticism focused on the taboo theme of miscegenation, an aspect of the novel that appeared to be of little concern in Boston.

From time to time, Miss Smith complained that the public had misinterpreted *Strange Fruit*, seeing in it themes that she had not intended. About a year after the book was published, she expressed her intentions in writing it: "I thought of my book as a fable about a son in search of a mother, about a race in search of surcease from pain and guilt—both finding what they sought in death and destruction." In 1949 she elaborated upon her intentions in her column in *The Chicago Defender*:

> I do not believe it is possible to understand the white man in America and his strange paranoid notions about his "superiority" without con-

sidering his equally strange childhood and the training he received before he was six-years-old, the heavy guilt laid on heart and body while both were so young and weak, and finally the strange fruit which this kind of training has borne, not only of White Supremacy but of mental illness, alcoholism, child delinquency, exploitation and war-making. That was what I tried to say in my novel published five years ago. The "strange fruit" I wrote of was not lynching or miscegenation (a word I hate) but the white man himself and his children and his Tobacco Roads and his own wasted life; the "strange fruit" was man dehumanized by a culture that is not good for the growth of either white or colored children. But quite a few people in their defensiveness saw it otherwise; some as a tract against lynching, and some as a libel on the Negro race, and some as a book against the South. It was strange to be at the receiving end of these reactions. I suppose truth is a three-edged knife that hurts everybody, especially the author!

Despite Miss Smith's disclaimer, the major theme in *Strange Fruit* involves the structure of a segregated society and the problems which that society breeds—the evils of racial segregation. Miss Smith despised separation of the races as one more artificial barrier between human beings. Regardless of the author's intentions, *Strange Fruit* had a propagandistic impact across the country. Northerners liked the book because it exposed the racial situation of the South; but some, as in Boston, vigorously condemned the book because of its language. Southerners, with their aversion for race-mixing, either condemned the book to the trash pile or ignored it. Like Harriet Beecher Stowe after the publication of *Uncle Tom's Cabin*, Lillian Smith became something of a celebrity in the North, where she was honored as a spokesman for integration of the races. She sometimes resented the fact that she was honored more as a spokesman than as a novelist or as an artist, but the record does not show that she accepted the role unwillingly.

III *Form and Style*

In form, *Strange Fruit*'s panoramic presentation of the people of Maxwell as puppets whose behavior is determined by society is in the classical tradition of Naturalism of the early works of Emile Zola. The novel covers the landscape of the town, with the spotlight on individuals in the Negro community, the middle-class white community, the mill town of the poor whites, and a nearby farm community. *Strange Fruit* touches upon all aspects of life from the real everyday business of making a living and maintaining a household to sexual fantasy, from abortion to bootleg whiskey. As Miss Smith stated many times in the course of her career, she liked a big novel that presented a whole picture of society. In writing *Strange Fruit*, she wrote to her own taste.

Miss Smith's sensational subject matter is presented in a style that is subdued in tone and that relies upon the plain language of the folk in a small Deep South town. The characters speak in the idiom of ordinary, uninspired people; the dialogue rings true; it is flat, dull, and unrevealing of character. If the Realism of the dialogue seems too pat for fiction, it should be remembered that Miss Smith was concerned with the walls which prevent communication between people. She saw all sorts of barriers to honesty in verbal communication. Her characters, then, say what they think is expected of them; or, in order to reassure others who may be more fearful, they say what will be comforting. They rarely reveal their true feelings in conversation. Regardless of the failure of verbal communication, all human beings have memories, dreams, and thoughts. And through her skillful use of flashback and stream-of-consciousness techniques Miss Smith portrays the most interesting aspects of her characters. When the novel was dramatized for Broadway, the flatness of the dialogue constituted an obvious flaw in the play.

As might be expected, Miss Smith's stylistic devices pleased some book reviewers while displeasing others. One of the most favorable reviews was written by Struthers Burt for *Saturday Review of Literature*. He summed up his evaluation of the work as follows: " 'Strange Fruit' is a major novel whatever else you may think of it. Firmly and convincingly written, with great strength and feeling and power, it is often eloquent."[3] Bernard DeVoto also praised the novel and its author: "A Southern woman has lately published a novel about the South. It is both a courageous novel and a good one, serious, mature, wise, excellently written."[4] Orville Prescott said: "It is written with much use of the stream of consciousness method and many deft time shifts. It is a very considerable achievement."[5]

Objections to the author's style were mainly directed at her violations of "good taste" and her "confusing" use of time. Joseph McSorley, reviewing the novel in *Catholic World*, objected to the author's use of time as a special device; but he also objected to the novel on the same grounds as the Boston Police Department: "One of the literary devices she employs—shifting from present tense to past and back again without warning—confuses the reader. Most important of all, presumably for the purpose of appealing to a vulgar multitude, she sins against good taste so grossly as to make her story quite unfit for general circulation. It seems curious enough that 'the daughter of one of the South's oldest families' should . . . employ phrases which decent people regard as unprintable." [6]

Cecelia Gaul said the book was "a little annoying in style," but she concluded that it might be "the most important novel of the year." [7] And the reviewer for the *Christian Science Monitor* thought that, "to many readers, the uncouth speech and licentious behavior" would be an affront." [8]

Despite the protestations of some reviewers, Lillian Smith was a master of her own variations upon the flashback and stream-of-consciousness techniques: and her shifts in time provide the relief in style that is essential to avoid tediousness. The depth of the novel is considerably enhanced by her skillful interweaving of past actions and thoughts with present situations to create an awareness of cause and effect. Miss Smith, who was convinced that the evils of segregation had their beginnings in psychological and sociological error, wanted her readers to become aware of the roots as well as the fruits of the racial dilemma. Through her stylistic devices, she achieved an economy of language with the result that *Strange Fruit* is a compact novel that, nevertheless, covers a large subject. She was not so successful in her later novel, *One Hour*.

IV *Characters*

Strange Fruit has a large cast of characters, many of whom are carefully and realistically drawn. Miss Smith's personal respect for the Negro people is reflected in her conception of Negro characters. In treating Negro characters with dignity, insight, and sympathy, she avoided the stereotypes of Negroes so frequent in American fiction. She succeeded in individualizing almost all of her characters even though she clearly intended to portray a cross-section of the population of a small Southern town. The plot involving miscegenation, however, tended to divert reader-critics from honest consideration of the book as literature at the time it was published. In the judgement of the Massachusetts Supreme Judicial Court, *Strange Fruit* has an average of one obscenity for every five pages. Edward Weeks, however, expressed a different view:

In its light and shade, in its violent contrasts, the book is absorbing
. . . . And here are other scenes so coarse in word and implication that
they are bound to offend. But despite the shock that is here, I find
nothing in the novel that is pornographic; the effect is not to make you
want to follow after Nonnie and Tracy. Without the shock, I doubt if
the moral would have gone home. At the speed things are moving
today, I suspect we shall be needing a new Uncle Tom's Cabin for each
decade. This one comes from the South, and this time New England
seems afraid of it.[9]

Tracy Deen serves as a symbol of the white South. He walks with
a limp, he is economically nonproductive, he is preoccupied with
his relationship to a Negro woman, and his behavior is determined
by social attitudes. He thus reflects Miss Smith's views regarding
the majority race in the South. Tracy is a passive figure whose death
hardly touches the reader: no feeling either for or against him flows
to the reader. Very likely this effect is what Miss Smith intended to
accomplish. It was because of love, not hate, for her region that she
wanted to expose the South's dilemma; and, while she hoped that
change would come, she counted upon reason, not strong feelings,
to prevail. When her intentions are viewed in this light, her objections to various interpretations of *Strange Fruit* as pornographic
propaganda are understandable.

In the tradition of characters in Naturalistic novels, Tracy's actions
are determined by outside factors, the social structure of Maxwell.
Even his decision to ask Henry to marry Nonnie was made upon
the advice of Brother Dunwoodie, a revivalist preacher, who said to
Tracy: "Find some good nigger you can count on to marry her.
Give her some money. They like money—all women like money,
no matter what color! Give him some money, too." The reader
obtains little insight into Tracy's feelings for Nonnie. He is momentarily incensed by the preacher's advice; but, under the influence
of his mother and Dunwoodie, he joins the church and tries to
implement the preacher's suggestion.

While the reader is revolted by Tracy's willingness to hire Henry
to marry Nonnie, it is obvious that having his servant marry her
would be the most likely way for him to keep Nonnie close enough
for his relationship with her to continue. There is no evidence, however, that Tracy thought of this factor, and the reader remains
convinced that he does not care enough for Nonnie to construct
such a plan. His behavior, then, is intended to portray the way such

matters are handled in a segregated society that forbids interracial marriage. In fact, the novel is not *about* him in any impelling way. His death occurs about two-thirds of the way through the novel, an event that leaves the author free to reveal what the novel is really about: a Southern town and segregation of the races.

Nonnie, like Tracy, is on the fringes of life. Although she has sacrificed whatever advantages her college education might have brought her to return to Maxwell and to domestic service to be near Tracy, the reader does not experience with her any overwhelming devotion to him. The reader is never convinced that what she does is *right*, as he is in the case of the "heroine" in D. H. Lawrence's *Lady Chatterley's Lover* or as he is in regard to the "heroines" of some of Tennessee Williams's plays, such as Lady Torrence in *Orpheus Descending*. Williams sees modern woman as attaining reality of existence only through a satisfactory sexual relationship, but Miss Smith does not offer any such compelling explanation for Nonnie's alliance with Tracy. When the novel opens, she is already pregnant. She is standing at the gate in the early darkness, waiting for Tracy and thinking: "Strange . . . being pregnant could make you feel like this. So sure. After all the years, Bess wouldn't see it. You hated to try to explain. Bess would feel disgraced. Ruined. The Andersons ruined, Bess would say." What else there is in Nonnie's feelings about her pregnancy and her man does not come through to the reader. She is speechless during Tracy's last visit when he tells her that he has arranged for Henry to marry her and when he leaves the money on the fence.

Nonnie lives in the old family home with her sister, Bess, and Bess's husband and young son. Bess, a well-drawn character, is involved with her husband, her child, her job, and the business of maintaining a home. She is proud of the Anderson family and name, and she has suffered in silence as Nonnie's affair with Tracy has progressed. Having long since accepted Nonnie as a dreamer whom she cannot understand, she, like various white people who are aware of the illicit relationship, acts as if she were not aware of it. But she takes charge of the situation immediately after Ed, having shot Tracy on the path, returns to the house. She knew "that the time had come for whispers."

Bess's mother, Tillie, who has died before the novel begins, had created a loving and secure home for her children, despite the ever-present hardships faced by her race in a segregated society. Her love, courage, and strength are made vivid to the reader through the memories of Bess and Ed. The parallel characterization of Tillie and Mrs. Deen is obvious. Accepting, as Miss Smith did, the idea that the Negro family in America is matriarchal, she was careful to make the reader aware of Tillie's stoic efforts to nurture and protect her children. On the other hand, Mrs. Deen, because of her neuroticism and inability to make satisfactory relationships, failed her children as a mother. While it is true that Tillie's son murdered Tracy, his act was one with which any self-respecting person could sympathize—because of Tracy's plans for Nonnie. Mrs. Deen's psychological characteristics, which Miss Smith claimed were at the heart of the novel, are discussed later in this chapter.

Dr. Sam, a physician, is a convincing character. He is the type of respected, hard-working, self-tormented professional Negro who may be found in almost any Negro community. He is in love with Nonnie, and the reader feels for him as he has to stand by and see the hopeless situation in which she is involved. A lifelong friend and confidant of the Anderson family, Dr. Sam, on the night of the murder, helps Ed to escape by driving him to Macon to catch a train for New York. Fatigue is a familiar feeling for Dr. Sam, who is constantly in the service of his fellow Negroes; in contrast, Dr. Deen is a passive, easygoing man who, for the most part, remains aloof from the intimate concerns of his family and friends. On moral grounds he declines to perform an abortion for the fourteen-year-old daughter of his close friend, L. D. Stephenson; but it is Mrs. Deen who keeps him from "going fishing too much and neglecting" his practice.

The minor characters in *Strange Fruit* are representative of the types that might be found in any small town. Redheaded Harriet Harris, whose father owns the mill and other businesses, is boldly outspoken about the quality of religion to be found in Maxwell, saying such things as "there's something immoral about a revival." Still, she is tolerated because of *who* she is. Her male counterpart, who is much older than Harriet, is Prentiss Reid, editor of the town newspaper and "Maxwell's radical." As might be expected, Reid does not publish his beliefs; instead, he conforms to the expectations of the power structure.

Epp Rushton, a rich bachelor, another type who may be found in almost any small town, lives alone in a fine house with his "books and nudist magazines and copies of great sculptures." He does not go to church, yet he is tolerated in Maxwell because of *who* he is and because he stays to himself. And Brother Dunwoodie, the revivalist, ex-sinner, ex-army man, ex-professional baseball player, is also typical of some Protestant ministers who have been "called" to preach and who may be found throughout the country.

Other minor characters include the man-sized town idiot, Crazy Carl; the long-suffering Mrs. Brown with her hydrocephalic child; a gossipy telephone operator; and Dessie, Henry's girl friend, an eager young Negro domestic servant. The poor, ignorant, oppressed, miserable, and hopeless whites of the milltown are ripe for violence at the least provocation; and the provocation comes in this instance from the dead body on the path to "colored town." The name of the victim is of no consequence, as long as he is white. These poor whites, who can relieve their tensions by lynching a Negro, according to Miss Smith and others, are guilt-ridden and fearful.

Miss Smith's analytical approach to characterization reflects her own keen observations as well as her extensive reading of modern psychology. As is often the case with the Naturalistic novel, the characters are presented realistically but without the infusion of feeling and emotion that compels strong reader identification with them. Despite Miss Smith's contention that many readers disliked *Strange Fruit* because they were forced "to identify . . . with a character or situation unflattering to self-esteem," the reader is more likely to *react* to what is happening to the characters than to experience emotional identification with them. But there is more than *reaction* in the appeal of the novel. Its power lies in the author's objective and unemotional dissection of the society of a small Southern town early in the twentieth century. The reader may be fascinated or repulsed by the operation, but he finds it difficult to turn away. Since Miss Smith, like Zola, Dreiser, and others, had a moralistic purpose in writing *Strange Fruit*, she undoubtedly wanted readers to react and then to take corrective action.

V *Psychological-Sociological Indictment*

In writing *Strange Fruit*, Lillian Smith obviously intended to reveal to the world *how it was* with both whites and blacks in Maxwell. She had already indicated in book reviews and critical notes in *South Today* and elsewhere that she favored the psychological-sociological approach to the writing of fiction. Thus, both her theoretical approach to the novel and her method in *Strange Fruit* support the conclusion that this novel is a psychological-sociological indictment of racial segregation. The work is successfully created in the tradition of Naturalism, even though it may be that, at this time, Miss Smith was not schooled in the theory of Naturalism as projected by Zola and others. She believed in it, nevertheless.

In her approach to characterization, Miss Smith inevitably drew upon her understanding of Freud and other theorists in modern psychology. Alma Deen, for instance, is portrayed as the only child of Reverend Mathews, a plodding Methodist preacher, and Rosa Mathews, a wealthy, carefree daughter of the Old South. Alma grows up believing that "Father would have been one of the big men in Southern Methodism had it not been for Mother's frivolous ways." Rosa, on the other hand, neither believes that her husband is "bishop material" nor wants to be the wife of a bishop. Thus Alma is so unlike her mother in both appearance and attitudes that her mother, a pretty and vivacious woman, finds it hard to believe that this serious young woman "with her plain face and her father's figure" is her child. The mother, who is frequently risqué, once says: "Every time I look at Alma I feel as if I've just read a chapter in the Bible and said my prayers."

Although Alma's father "seemed to enjoy" her mother's lively behavior, Alma develops an aversion for all that her mother does and says. She develops strong sympathies for her father, believing as she does that he is a victim of her mother's frivolity. Because she thinks her mother has failed to help her father in his career, she vows, at the time of her marriage, "that she would be a *real* wife to Tut, helping him with his career." Lying beside her husband many years later, she reassures herself that

> She had been a good wife to Tut, submitting to his embraces quietly, without protest—though that part of marriage seemed to Alma a little unclean and definitely uncomfortable; helping him with his practice; collecting the fees which Tut would never have collected; saving, investing; running a smooth home; carefully taking his calls; keeping Tut from going fishing too much and neglecting a practice that had grown large through the years. Always remembering Mother, Alma had urged Tut on. (64)

After the birth of her first baby, Tracy, Mrs. Deen is a happy, devoted mother until her own mother comes to see the grandchild. As always, Rosa Mathews has the effect of destroying Alma's sense of well-being and of causing her to take diametrically opposed views. Rosa Mathews is attracted to the baby immediately. "He'll be full of spirit," she says. "He could be my very own." After picking up the baby, she looks at her daughter and says, "I must admit that you've done a much better job on your first-born than I did!" After these words, Alma "stood there, looking at the baby in her mother's arms, and cried, 'I don't want it,' she said in her bitterness, and turned away. 'I don't want him,' she cried, and knew that she meant her words." Afterward, she feels that Tracy belongs more to her mother than to her. When she becomes pregnant again, Alma allows her mother to take Tracy home with her where he presumably stays until the day when Rosa Mathews "laughed so heartily that she dropped dead." This rejection of Tracy by Mrs. Deen undoubtedly prompted Miss Smith's statement that the book was "about a son in search of a mother."

Because of her maladjustment to her mother, Alma Deen's behavior is frequently motivated by the desire to be different or to prove her mother wrong. For instance, "she was convinced that her own mother's custom of sleeping in a room separate from Father's had caused their family to be not as successful as it should have been." Alma, therefore, insists upon sleeping in the bed with Tut. One night as she lies beside him, she thinks:

> Sometimes all she could remember of hers and Tut's nights together was the lifting of his leg off her body. There was something almost *dissipated* about the way Tut slept, letting himself go, so, so uncontrolled, you might say. Alma had thought of twin beds but had never done anything about it, for she doubted in her heart that husbands and wives should sleep separately. It was all a little vague to her, but sleeping together, cold weather or hot, seemed a necessary thread in the fabric of marriage, which, once broken, might cause the whole thing to unravel. (62)

Dr. Deen, in the manner of complacent husbands who have long since accepted the strange ways of their wives, tolerates Mrs. Deen without much thought or effort. When he does think of her, he visualizes a white cow. His association of Mrs. Deen with the white cow occurs to him one day when he is driving on a country road: "A big, white cow had clambered up in the middle of the road and had stood gazing at him unwaveringly, and he had thought: 'Now if that ain't Alma all over' " (124).

When Alma's mother shows almost no interest in Laura, the second grandchild, Alma devotes herself to her daughter. And Laura, during her early years, adores her mother and confides in her. As Laura grows up, however, Mrs. Deen's attitude toward her borders on incestuous fantasy. After Laura leaves for college, Mrs. Deen sometimes sleeps in her bed to avoid her husband. As her mother grows more and more possessive of her, Laura realizes "that her mother had discarded her own life, as you throw away a dress you don't like, and had chosen to live hers instead. . . . It was as if, having once nourished Laura within her body, she now claimed an equal right to feed upon her whom she had brought to life" (190).

When Laura evinces an interest in art, Mrs. Deen slips into her room to destroy her clay and a clay figure, so that Laura can only conclude that *"she hates what I like."* Later Mrs. Deen searches Laura's desk and reads some letters Laura has received from Jane Hardy, an unmarried schoolteacher. Although Laura's affection for Jane indicates tendencies toward homosexuality, Mrs. Deen implies that such a relationship exists when, in fact, there has been no overt behavior on the part of the two women. Her warning to Laura, however, about a possible homosexual relationship, has the effect of disgusting Laura and of destroying her feeling for her friend.

Mrs. Deen's psychological effect upon Tracy's emotional development is less clear-cut than the author apparently intended it to be or than it is upon Laura. The question arises as to whether Mrs. Deen's early rejection of Tracy can account for all of his psychological problems. Some of his characteristics are his lack of ego, his lack of motivation in life, his inability to make lasting relationships with his peers, his lack of moral direction, and his malleability at the hands of his mother and Reverend Dunwoodie. He does not have the high level of enjoyment in life that his grandmother had, nor does he have the ambition of his mother. He also lacks the philosophical patience of his father. Tracy does not appear to have an unusual attachment to his mother; neither does he appear to harbor hostility toward her.

Once, late at night, when Tracy stops by his sister's room to chide her for her lack of heterosexual relationships, he reveals a somewhat crude pleasure in sex. After the little conversational exchange, he throws "back his head and laughed softly, and his teeth . . . flashed in the lamplight." Never having seen him in this mood before, Laura momentarily thinks that she understands why he appeals to the "Negro girl" and to other types, such as "all the Miss Belles, the old maids, the young married, and the very old ladies." She believes they want "to soothe him." This fleeting insight into Tracy's personality does not, however, adequately support Miss Smith's contention that Tracy is searching for mother love, brought about by Alma's rejection of him, when he establishes his liaison with Nonnie Anderson. In the absence of a strong identification with his mother, such as might inhibit a sexual relationship with a woman from his mother's social class, the reader is left to assume that his lack of ego causes him to seek a sexual mate whom he and his society consider "inferior" to him.

On another level, Tracy Deen, with his lame foot and his lack of ambition, may be construed as a symbol of a decadent white South and its involvement with the Negro race. This interpretation supports Miss Smith's statement that she was writing "about a race in search of surcease from pain and guilt." Yet, as Miss Smith knew, Tracy's lack of ambition, and by analogy the South's "lack of progress," could not be wholly attributed to involvement with the black race. Knowing this fact, she realized that no simplistic analogue was available for portrayal of the South's problems. As mentioned previously, she insisted upon portraying poverty, ignorance, and religion as complicating factors.

Nevertheless, the psychological problems that evolved in the biracial South were of more interest to Miss Smith than the economic problems that have been of prime interest to many sociologists. Only briefly, in depicting the poor whites of milltown, does Miss Smith touch upon the economic situation of Maxwell and, by extension, of the whole South. One white laborer complains that Tom Harris pays him "exactly enough to starve on." When one of the women remarks, "If they warn't so many niggers, might be folks would git more money," she receives the answer that the "way they streaking North now won't soon be no niggers." The seeds of the economic conditions of the region are in the novel, but they are not of major concern to the author.

The failure of communication between individuals and between the races is of major concern to Lillian Smith. In *Strange Fruit*, the lack of honest and sincere communication is pronounced in the characterization of Mrs. Deen, who is almost mute in the presence of her husband and children. No member of the Deen family tries to understand another or to be understood by another. Even the members of the Anderson family, who love and protect each other, cannot communicate with each other verbally. And honest communication between the races is an impossibility in Maxwell. In a conversation with Tom Harris just before the lynching, Dr. Sam fabricates an alibi for Henry McIntosh. When Harris asks Dr. Sam why he has lied, Dr. Sam answers that he had to. Then he observes: "Because a Negro can't afford the truth! Truth's for powerful folks." The other side of this situation is that a majority race that requires dishonesty on the part of a minority ceases to respect or even to recognize truth and honesty, either in its own interpersonal relationships or in interracial matters.

Even though Tracy and Nonnie persist in their sexual relations, there is no evidence that in the sexual act the partners find a means of full communication as do some of the characters in the plays of Tennessee Williams. In *Strange Fruit*, sex is represented as something unclean in the thinking of genteel ladies, something to be joked about by vulgar old men and girl watchers, and something to be enjoyed surreptitiously by such couples as Tracy and Nonnie or Henry and Dessie. In the context of this novel, sex provides some escape from the humdrum daily life, but it does not substitute for verbal communication by strengthening marital relationships, heightening awareness and sensitivity, or releasing anxiety.

In real life, tragedy frequently produces an intimacy among family members and among friends that may have been absent before. In the case of the Deen family, no such intimacy occurs, even when their only son is murdered on the path leading to his black mistress. Thus, the failure of communication is not resolved. The walls between individuals and races do not crumble. And the implication is that the dishonesty that permeates private and public life in Maxwell is the product, or the "strange fruit," of racial segregation.

VI *Irony*

As Fred Marcus has pointed out in his comparison of *Strange Fruit* with Alan Paton's *Cry, the Beloved Country*, "Lillian Smith uses irony—ranging from mild to acid—as one means of creating tension, tension as volatile as the flaring up of race violence."[10] The supreme irony in *Strange Fruit* is inherent in the connivance of Mrs. Deen and Reverend Dunwoodie to influence Tracy to desert his pregnant mistress, join the church, and marry an innocent young woman whom he does not love. By accepting the advice of the two people who most want to save him, Tracy is killed, not saved. Furthermore, Mrs. Deen's money, which Tracy had delivered to Nonnie, enables Tracy's murderer to escape.

There is bitter irony in the lynching of Henry McIntosh, the harmless, innocent, and devoted friend of Tracy, for Tracy's murder. It is through Henry's friendly willingness to marry Nonnie that Tracy is to be relieved of responsibility. Yet this black friend fears to report the finding of Tracy's body because he realizes he will be accused of the murder.

Irony also derives from the double standard of morality that is the result of segregation and of religious sanction of it. Members of the white community, in the words of Prentiss Reid, support Christianity but do not practice it. In every situation, therefore, where whites assume themselves to be morally superior, the blacks prove themselves to be superior. The Deen family, for instance, fails to coalesce, even in an hour of tragedy; but the Andersons remain tolerant, understanding, and supportive of each other in their troubles.

Contrasting moral attitudes are exposed in the case of two illegitimate pregnancies. Nonnie's pregnancy is a result of her love for Tracy, whom she would have married if white morality had allowed it. Nevertheless, she and her family will accept and love her baby. On the other hand, when Grace Stephenson, a young white girl, becomes pregnant by Mart Paine, her father is willing to go to any effort and expense to obtain an abortion for her. According to the father, Mart Paine is "white trash"; and he will not let his daughter, who is not yet fifteen years old, marry him. Dr. Deen refuses to perform the abortion, saying "If a nigger had raped her it'd be different—it'd be different, but—but this was—she did it for fun—for fun with a boy she liked." He does, however, suggest a doctor in Atlanta who will perform the abortion. By comparison, Nonnie's love for Tracy is on a mature and sincere plane, while the behavior of Grace Stephenson is licentious.

In the view of Miss Smith, the effects of social segregation as a repressive force upon the black minority are obvious to those who are willing to acknowledge them, but the damage to the white majority has not always been so readily recognizable. By her effective use of situational irony, achieved through a bare, realistic

style, the author makes her point, unequivocally, that racial prejudice and social segregation cut two ways. The social structure, as
devised by the white majority for its own protection and well-being,
serves as a destructive force upon the moral and social fabric of
white society. Miss Smith's success in conveying this truth through
the use of irony provides much of the power and the shock of
Strange Fruit.

VII *Unity*

Unity is achieved in *Strange Fruit* through structure and characterization. The dominant theme of social determinism is the perva-
sive element that binds each scene to the other as the panorama
unrolls before the reader. Through the author's use of memory,
reverie, and stream-of-consciousness techniques, the cause and
effect of the current situation in Maxwell are emphasized and thus
serve to strengthen the unity of the thematic structure. In the
closed society of Maxwell, the lives of all of the residents black and
white, poor and rich, old and young,—are so interwoven that any
disturbance on the social surface nudges everybody into a defensive
posture. In view of the toppling domino effect of events and the
ironic results of moral actions that thread the novel from beginning
to end, it is difficult to grasp the critical point made by Francis
Downing. After praising Miss Smith's understanding and clarifica-
tion of the race conflict in the South, he drew the following conclusion: "Yet, somehow, in the world of realities and of ideas the
novel tends to fall to pieces in her hands. She seems to be saying
that men live by symbols, and that if we but change the symbols
all is well."[11] The opposite, of course, is true: Miss Smith wanted
an end to segregation of the races, not through a change of symbols,
but through human growth and social development. *Strange Fruit*
is her statement, and it does not "fall to pieces."

The characterization of Nonnie Anderson strengthens the unity
of the novel. She appears on the first page: "She stood at the gate,
waiting; behind her, the swamp, in front of her, Colored Town,
beyond it, all Maxwell." Her image casts a silent shadow on every
page of the novel, until finally, on the last page, she puts on her
white oxfords to return to her job on the morning after the lynching.
The taut thread of life in Maxwell, after a spasm of violence, is
intact. And so is the novel.

VIII *On Broadway*

Apparently the author who has been to Broadway and failed has
a great deal to remember, a cache of experience that cannot be
gained elsewhere and bruises to the ego which life can seldom heal.
With all of Miss Smith's gift for ferreting out answers to her own
questions, she never resolved to her own satisfaction the causes of
her failure on Broadway. The immediate public success of her novel
seemed to promise success on Broadway for a play based on the
same material. In the spring of 1944, therefore, Miss Smith signed
a contract with José Ferrer to produce *Strange Fruit* on Broadway.
The plan was that Lillian and her sister, Esther Smith, would col-
laborate in writing the script. Esther, who had had a great deal of
experience in producing and directing college plays, had valuable
knowledge of technical aspects of the theater. She took a two-year
leave of absence from her teaching position to assist Lillian in
writing the play. Later she played the part of a minor character in
the novel, Miss Belle, a white spinster seamstress who lived on the
borderline between whites and blacks and who made her living
sewing for both.

In the fall of 1944, the two sisters moved into an apartment in the
Hotel Margaret in Brooklyn Heights, an apartment that Lillian
maintained until 1953. Together, they began the long process of
converting the novel into drama. Although all of Lillian Smith's
drafts of the play, correspondence, records, and other paraphernalia
were destroyed by fire in 1955, she recalled that the first draft of
the play was intended to be staged without curtains. There would
have been one set with portions of the stage to be lighted at different times, somewhat similiar to the staging used in Arthur
Miller's *Death of a Salesman*. The playwrights contended that this
stage technique would accelerate the action since there would be
no breaks, there would be no time lost in changing sets, and there
would be no noise backstage (in the final staging, backstage noise
caused by many scene changes was a problem). The producers objected that the idea was experimental and risky, and Lillian Smith
and José Ferrer, who was the director as well as one of the producers,
acceded to those who raised such objections. The play was rewritten
to be produced in the traditional manner with scene changes.[12]

An examination of the only available copy of the play, a mimeo-
graphed one on deposit at the New York Public Library,[13] revealed

that the script followed the novel closely, having two acts, twelve scenes, and eleven scene changes, as follows:

Act I:

Scenes 1 and 5—Deen's Drug Store

Scene 2—Anderson's Home

Scene 3—Deen's Sun Porch

Scene 4—The Ridge

Act II:

Scenes 1 and 2—Deen's Yard

Scene 3—Salamander's Cafe

Scenes 4 and 6—Anderson's Gate

Scene 5—Deen's Sun Porch

Scene 7—Tom Harris' Mill Office

The completed manuscript called for thirty-four characters; and the final production, according to Miss Smith, required some thirty-five stagehands. Casting, which took place over a period of several months, demanded considerable energy on the part of the director and the playwrights. Finally, Melchor Ferrer was chosen for the part of Tracy; and Jane White, daughter of Walter White of the National Association for the Advancement of Colored People, was selected for the part of Nonnie. Jane White, according to Miss Smith, took the role over the objections of her father who did not like either the novel or the play. Eugenia Rawls created the role of Harriet Harris, and Juano Hernandez played the part of Dr. Sam Perry. George Jenkins designed the sets; Patricia Montgomery, the costumes.

The plan was to open the play in Montreal, then move to Toronto, Boston, and Philadelphia before opening on Broadway. When it opened in Montreal, the play ran to four hours; but, in spite of its excessive length, Lillian Smith recalled that it was well received. As the play progressed through the other cities, the authors worked at shortening it by an hour. *Strange Fruit* opened on Broadway at the Royale Theatre on November 29, 1945; it closed on January 19, 1946.

Various factors undoubtedly contributed to the failure of the play, the most likely being the lack of experience of the playwrights and the nature of the novel from which they worked. The panoramic small-town atmosphere, the flat idiom of rural people, and the large number of minor characters, while effective in the novel, were too literally transferred to the stage. In this connection, Rosamond

Gilder, writing in *Theatre Arts*, had mixed reactions to the play.

> It is a relief to come upon a play which, while obviously deficient in
> its playwriting techniques and not by any means uniformly effective
> on the production level, is rich in matter, in humanity and in emotion.
> Lillian Smith's *Strange Fruit* has not completely emerged from novel
> into theatre; it is a series of dialogues rather than a march of events;
> its linked movements fail to reach the crisis inherent in its story. Yet
> with all its faults of structure it is so rich in content and so moving in
> presentation that it out-distances many a better-made play.[14]

Stark Young said that *Strange Fruit* was true to the South but not
"expertly done." He praised the George Jenkins sets but complained
about Ferrer's directing.[15]

In spite of Lillian Smith's apprehension about the staging, and her
later regrets that she had not insisted upon her experimental
approach, others in addition to Young praised the sets. George Jean
Nathan thought the sets were "atmospherically interesting,"[16] and
Miss Gilder described the set, after calling attention to the dual
lines of the play—the love of the protagonists within the "vast, ill-
adjusted social order":

> To express this dual plane of action, José Ferrer as producer and
> director and George Jenkins as designer have set the play in a series
> of small scenes set against a larger panorama. The village street runs
> past the drug store, the mill office, the cafe. Back of the Anderson's
> cabin loom the tall trees of a dismal swamp; the lovers meet on a high
> place by the bend of a river. The village street scenes are used effec-
> tively to indicate the ebb and flow of town life, the clotting antagonisms,
> the sharp distinctions and animosities that build toward open war.
> Unfortunately the technical difficulties of this multiple-set method are
> not entirely overcome in the production. There sometimes seems to be
> more scene-shifting than scene and the mechanics interfere with the
> establishment of mood. In themselves, however, the sets are imagina-
> tive and evocative.[17]

George Jean Nathan, who did not find much in the production of
Strange Fruit that pleased him, wrote:

> The play is clearly the work of a novice in dramaturgy and accord-
> ingly misses what effect the novel had. Yet were it a play infinitely
> better it would still not seem so in the production here accorded it.

Mr. Ferrer has staged it in so monotonous a manner, has pitched its tone for the most part so low, and has allowed it so much inaudibility that there are moments when the audience does not know whether it is itself or the actors who are asleep. In such waking moments as there are, it further can not make out, with the stagehands' thunderous backstage racket, if what it is seeing is a dramatization of *Strange Fruit* or a revival of *Shenandoah.* Considering the doldrums of the exhibit in the more frequent other moments, it probably might not have been a bad idea to have the actors and stagehands change places.[18]

Both Nathan and Gilder praised Jane White's appearance and sensitivity in this her first Broadway role, but they both thought she needed more experience. Miss Gilder also praised Melchor Ferrer's performance and Lillian Smith's characterization of Tracy Deen:

In her play as in her novel, Miss Smith gives her people substance and reality; she sees into the complex inner pressures that make them individually what they are and beyond them to the large forces that sweep them helplessly to disaster. So her weakling-hero comes to life on the stage in Melchor Ferrer's excellent interpretation, as a preordained victim of his environment—emotionally unstable, incapable of action, escaping the harsher demands of discipline in the kindly, protective bosom of his Negro mammy, the companionship of his adoring boyhood friend and servant Henry, and in the devotion of his beloved.[19]

Perhaps a minor factor in the short run of *Strange Fruit* was the presence of another play on the theme of Negro-white relations on Broadway. This play, *Deep Are the Roots*, by Arnaud d'Usseau and James Gow, opened on September 26, 1945, some two months ahead of *Strange Fruit. Deep Are the Roots,* which reversed the situation of *Strange Fruit* by depicting a white girl in love with a Negro man, was drawing capacity crowds when Miss Smith's play opened. The cast of characters for *Deep Are the Roots* included Barbara Bel Geddes in the role of Genevra Langdon with Gordon Heath as Brett Charles; Elia Kazan was the director. Critics, who generally praised the acting and the directing, concluded that *Deep Are the Roots* was more expertly constructed than *Strange Fruit.* Thus it seems plausible that, as Miss Smith was firmly convinced, *Deep Are the Roots,* by getting to Broadway first, diminished the interest in *Strange Fruit.*

In any event, only modest audiences materialized, and *Strange Fruit* was in trouble from the beginning. With such a large cast and with so many stagehands, the payroll for the production was so exorbitant that meeting it would have required, for a long run, a full house at almost every performance. Toward the end of December, after notice had been given that the play would close the first week in January, Lillian Smith learned that she had accumulated, as her share of the proceeds, some fifteen thousand dollars. On New Year's Eve, therefore, she had a party for the cast and included the stagehands, notwithstanding the fact that she felt that the stagehands, for some antagonistic reason, had deliberately tried to destroy the play with their backstage noise. At the party, Miss Smith announced that she was putting her share of the proceeds back into the play to keep it running as long as possible. Even so, the play closed on January 19, 1946.

For an author who was still riding the crest of her fame over the publication of the novel, the closing of *Strange Fruit* on Broadway was a traumatic experience. Her tendency to blame the play's failure on outside factors and on others involved in the production, rather than on the script prepared by her and her sister, is evidence of her strong personality and possibly of her inability to cooperate in the close teamwork necessary for successful playwriting and production. Also, in view of Lillian's somewhat domineering personality, it is not likely that her sister exerted much influence on the final script. The novel belonged to Lillian alone, and the play must be largely attributed to her. Although her experience on Broadway would have been better forgotten, she found it difficult to put it out of her mind. Wisely, perhaps, she never made the return journey.

CHAPTER *4*

One Hour

I N 1959, Lillian Smith published *One Hour*, her second novel. During the fifteen years between the publication of *Strange Fruit* and *One Hour*, she had published three nonfiction books; written and seen her play produced; contributed articles and made speeches on the problems of the South; traveled to India twice; and fought a six-year battle with cancer. When *One Hour* did appear, however, it proved to be a "big," panoramic novel to which Miss Smith had devoted the maximum of energy and conviction. She was concerned, as in the previous novel, with contemporary problems in American society. Although Windsor Hills, the town in *One Hour*, is supposed to be a Southern town and appears to be located in Virginia, probably near Washington, the events in that town and in the novel could have occurred in numerous towns throughout the United States.

One Hour was Miss Smith's response to the hysteria generated throughout the country by the witch hunts of the Senator Joseph McCarthy era. As Miss Smith wanted above all else to remove the barriers that separate people, she watched with horror as new walls of fear and suspicion were constructed by demagogues for their own selfish purposes. In *One Hour* the hysteria begins when eight-year-old Susan Newell, prodded by her mother, accuses a prominent scientist of attempted rape. Actually, the child had gone into an empty store where she was probably scratched by a cat; but, while she was in the semidarkness of the room, Mark Channing, the scientist, wandered into the building for no apparent reason; and the child saw him. Matters are complicated by the fact that Channing does not admit, for several weeks, that he had been in the building where the child was. Gossip and suspicion thrive among the ignorant, the idle, and the frustrated citizens of Windsor Hills. Finally, after an anonymous letter is sent to Channing's son, Andy, at preparatory school in New England, the boy wanders out into a snow storm and dies. After the lives of Channing and his wife are ruined, the charges are dropped; and the Channings move away to start over.

I *Narrative Techniques*

The point of view in *One Hour* is first person; and the narrator is an Episcopal minister, David Landrum, a bachelor, thirty-eight years old. Landrum, a devoted friend of both Channings, is also in love with Mrs. Channing. Since he is intended to be the epitome of the intellectual priest, he is immersed in Freudian psychology; in modern theological ideas, as represented by Reinhold Niebuhr and Paul Tillich; and in the latest thinking on art, music, and literature. He is also knowledgeable about food, drink, and other amenities of the civilized life. Since he represents Miss Smith's ideal preacher of the gospel, he knows as much about contemporary ideas and life as his parishioners.

In *Strange Fruit*, religion and preachers were portrayed at their realistic worst as hypocritical and as failing as forces for the good of human society. But, the reader familiar with Miss Smith's writing through the years, including her articles in *South Today*, has to accept Landrum, the ideal minister, as her spokesman. She was, herself, something of a minister of the gospel. That she saw herself in such a role is evident in the repitition of her ideas of what was "right" and "good" as opposed to what was "wrong" or "evil." In print, she frequently raised the question as to why people do not see that what they are doing is wrong, evil. At the same time that Landrum is saying the things which Miss Smith would have said, he serves multiple roles in the novel: he is priest, psychoanalyst, sociologist, and friendly counselor.

David Landrum, who lost a leg in World War II, is a partial man; and he is, therefore, only partially effective in his role as an intellectual priest. (It will be recalled that Tracy Dean in *Strange Fruit* walked with a limp.) At any rate, Landrum is guilty of committing the same sins as his parishioners; but he is aware of his guilt and thrashes himself with it. His human frailty becomes obvious when, after the death of young Andy and at a time of extreme anxiety in the Channing family, he commits adultery with Grace Channing.

When Landrum begins recalling events of his narrative, the action has been completed and the Channings have been gone from the town for two years. Landrum's musings, back and forth and roundabout, are illustrative of Lillian Smith's elliptical thinking which plagued her nonfiction works. As it turns out, *Strange Fruit* is the most objective of her books. More and more, as time passed, she placed herself at the center of her works since she was seemingly unable to maintain an objective stance in fiction or nonfiction. To some extent, she explained the back-and-forth motion which one finds in her writings; for, about the time *Strange Fruit* was published, she wrote in *South Today* as follows:

> It is the gaps in time that we find so hard to pull together. We have mastered space more successfully. Our imaginations encompass the globe with ease. But how many of us are able to travel backward forty, thirty, twenty, even ten years to the beginning of today's dilemma? Or to travel ahead and see the result of today's decision? This ability to swing through time, back and forth at will, is a skill most of us are curiously inept at. We refuse to accept cause and result as part of reality if the span of time is wide. We refuse to shape decisions to the curve that past and present and future make. The bending of time . . . we do not believe in it. Past and future meet . . . we turn away, we will not look at the meeting.

Her narrative deliberately illustrates her own thinking and how she thought civilized beings should observe themselves and their universe. In *One Hour*, Reverend Landrum performs as Miss Smith wished him to, even though his musings go on too long and the action is weakened by them.

One pitfall, of course, in meditating upon one set of events for years at a time is that the person who mediates wants to accuse someone, to place the blame for what happened. What is going to happen, as far as the narrator is concerned, is inherent in the first two paragraphs of *One Hour*:

> The most obvious thing about this hour is that it refuses to stay in its place in time. As I reach for minutes, I find years stretching back endlessly. When I search for its beginning, for that first tick of the first second, I hear only hearts beating.
>
> And yet, for a long time, I felt compelled to keep at it: I must find that elusive beginning, I must find who started it. Surely someone was to blame for what happened! But the beginning only slipped further back each time I grasped it, and the face of the scapegoat kept changing as I formed name after name in my mind.

The question of who is to blame for America's psychological and sociological problems concerned Lillian Smith during most of her adult life. Her question, even allowing for the most profound effort, can be answered only partially. Chasing the same question in search of *the* answer for thirty years or more leads, inevitably, to elliptical thinking, as Miss Smith realized at various times and as she had Landrum conclude on the first page of *One Hour*: "There is no end to this kind of thinking which is not thinking at all, of course, but only a most human try at unraveling stone."

As a character, Landrum sometimes irks the reader by taking pains to show that he and the Channings were "in" as intellectuals. The Channings, for instance, owned a Jackson Pollock painting. As Landrum helped Grace pack books after the catastrophe, he let the reader know that only the *right* books, the ones any pretender to intellectualism would have, were on the shelves. These were carefully listed: Dylan Thomas was there, of course, along with numerous others, including Ezra Pound, St. John Perse, André Gide, Franz Kafka, T. S. Eliot, Jean-Paul Sartre, Albert Camus, Henry James, and "the Dostoevskys." Then there were Kierkegaards and "a bright new copy of Dante—and . . . eight or ten of Freud's books and four or five of Jung's and one of Ferenczi's and two Ranks and Ernest Jones—now her art books, ten or twelve Skiras, *The Tao of Painting, The Art of Indian Painting.*" At this point, Landrum tells the reader, "I began to feel we were packing up our own era."

The whole atmosphere of Landrum's life is, by design, characterized by a middle-class intellectualism which he relishes beyond believability in such scenes as the following, which occurs shortly after Mark Channing's tragic loss of his son: "Mark brought in the drinks and we sat at the kitchen table while the steaks broiled and I worked on the salad. We didn't say much but the old feeling between us was right. My brain knew better but I felt, things are going to be as they once were; somehow, this other will level off; we'll talk again as we used to—and some day, Grace will sit here again listening, looking at us, feeling with each of us. . . . I remembered that we had always talked at our best, and now and then even with eloquence, when she was listening" (334).

On several counts, *One Hour* demands comparison with Alan Paton's second novel, *Too Late the Phalarope*. Both novels have the first-person narrators who are searching for the causes of what happened. Both novels have intellectual policemen as characters.

One Hour

In *One Hour*, Neel, the special assistant to the chief of police, holds a doctor's degree in clinical psychology from Columbia University and asks questions about St. John Perse. Both novels are constructed around charges of socially unacceptable sex acts. Again, the difference in the achievements of the two authors lies in their divergent approaches to fiction writing. Miss Smith undertook a Naturalistic dissection of the human condition, including as many aspects of the contemporary scene over a large span of time as could possibly be worked into one book. Paton's work has the lyrical quality of a birdsong, and it remains on key with attention focused upon the central problem.

II *Determinism and Thematic Development*

While *One Hour* is in the Naturalistic tradition, it differs from *Strange Fruit* in that the determinism results from man's inner drives. As indicated earlier, the structure of the segregated society in *Strange Fruit* is largely responsible for the psychological problems of the individual characters. In *One Hour*, the behavior of the characters is determined by deep psychological frustrations which result in such emotions as anxiety, fear, guilt, hate, love, persecution, and sexual obsession. This behavior, in turn, gives rise to complicated social problems. The enveloping theme of this novel depicts man as being at the mercy of his unconscious drives; the psychic recesses of the mind are explored to explain what happens in Windsor Hills. And, because of Miss Smith's notion of the "big" novel, the probing of the subconscious minds of a number of people between the ages of eight and eighty becomes a seemingly endless process. Reverend Landrum is the analyst who does the probing, but some small contributions come from the Channings, Neel, and even Claud Newell, one of his parishioners and the father of Susan.

Aside from the charges of attempted rape against Mark Channing in *One Hour*, there are various other descriptions and reports of sexual acts that seem to have been thrown in only for shock effect. Even though one must concede that Miss Smith, long under the Freudian influence, had a right to her notions of the essentiality of sexual acts and images in the lives and thoughts of her characters, some of the gratuitous sexual material in *One Hour* is included simply because the author was aware that such things have occurred in the experience of man and because her idea of the "big" novel encompassed all experience. It is paradoxical, however, that Miss

Smith should have relied so heavily on all forms of sex in her fiction when she was critical of the same inclusiveness in other writers. In reference to Hemingway's *For Whom the Bell Tolls*, for instance, she made the following comment: "As for Hemingway's adolescent fantasy of brawn and bawd, there isn't, of course, an idea in the book, but there is plenty of you-know-what, and the thing should appeal mightily to some very young men and some very old ones; but I should think from every woman over fifteen, it would only draw a broad smile and a broader yawn."[2]

In developing the major theme, the author emphasizes the conscious and subconscious sexual preoccupations of her characters. A brief résumé of the behavior of the various members of the family of little Susan Newell illustrates the ramifications of such a technique. To begin with, Susan's maternal grandfather, old Congressman Addams, had been known to have sexual relations with Negro women on the plantation. When Susan's mother Renie and her twin brother Ronie were eighteen years old, their father sexually abused a twelve- or thirteen-year-old Negro girl in a woodhouse near the family home. Mrs. Addams found the girl there; and, rather than believe that her husband was guilty of such an act, she chose to believe that her innocent son, Ronie, was the offender. As a result of the incident, Mrs. Addams gradually, over a period of one month, ceased to talk. At the time of the story, Congressman Addams has been dead a year or so; but his wife, who has not spoken for fifteen years, survives. Ronie, now an alcoholic, continues to live on the plantation with his mother. Mose Addams, a Negro who is actually Ronie's cousin, is in full charge of the plantation.

Renie, now married to Claud Newell, is reminiscent of Mrs. Deen in *Strange Fruit* in that she has fastidious notions about the sexual act. Renie's husband, in a long talk with Landrum, describes her as follows:

> Like a lot of other carefully brought up American girls she thinks there is only one way, one nice way, you know. But I happen to be different. There're a dozen ways, maybe a hundred ways. To hear our GI's talk when they come back from the Pacific. . . . But for my wife, there is only one right way. Where she learned it, I don't know. The lady who is her mother would never have mentioned even the word *sex*, to her. The point is, what she has decided is the right way is not right for me. And all this has really got big since her father's death. She flatly refuses my way.

One Hour

Previously Renie had told Landrum that her husband was impotent; but Newell, a traveling salesman, has another explanation. He tells Landrum: "A man can be in love with his wife and at the same time need something that only another woman can give him. A woman he doesn't love is exactly what he wants and must have, sometimes. Sex doesn't have anything to do with love and never has had. Because you are a minister and believe this is wrong does not keep it from being true." Newell, of course, does not fully realize that this modern, Freudian-oriented minister is quite capable of responding in kind. Landrum's reply is as follows:

> I won't debate the wrongness with you. We'd have to go too deep into things. But I will question its truth. A man may want—what he needs he's not willing to face up to—exactly what you say: somebody he can depersonalize, use, throw away afterward; or some nice little toy he can play with in childish ways and keep going back to because she lets him be the little boy he really is; or maybe what he wants is not a woman at all but a boy or a man but he's unwilling to admit it, so he takes a woman he can turn into a boy in his fantasy and use—and it never gets him anywhere—never satisfies him and never will—"

Somewhat taken aback by the minister's assessment of him, Newell then seriously begins to discuss his wife, who had apparently provoked Susan into accusing Dr. Channing of attempted rape. Newell thinks that "something is going on in Renie's mind about Channing. He fascinates her; his brilliance—now I know: I remember what brought it up: he spoke last summer on a health program. . . . Dr. Channing was speaking on cancer. Afterward Renie said quite a bit about his brilliance, his brains, that he was amazingly photogenic on television. Yet, she seems to hate him."

Later, after Andy Channing's death, Reverend Landrum relates the events culminating in the charges against Dr. Channing to Mr. Eliot, Andy's housemaster. From what the housemaster has heard from Landrum, Eliot assumes that the child Susan had arrived home with a scratch on her arm and that, after questioning her, the mother "did the linking" with Channing. Landrum then remarks: "Did she? You see, I'm not sure. Something in her did it, maybe. But if it did, this made it worse because something else in her did not want it: it acted like powerful enzymes, expediting, accelerating the destructive elements of her nature—She loves Susan as she hates her; loves and hates Claud, loves and fears her mother, loves and hates her dead father, and Ron, her twin brother. That's the family picture."

III *Psychological-Sociological Indictment*

In a final analysis, *One Hour* is less optimistic than *Strange Fruit*. In the first novel, society is the culprit; and the implication is that society can be changed by laws, by religious leaders, and by well-meaning political and social leaders. In *One Hour*, however, the underlying message is that each individual, being human, has deep psychological motivations which he does not understand and seemingly cannot control or change. These motivations, which derive from sexual frustrations, cause bizarre and unexplainable behavior. For example, even the highly respected Dr. Channing becomes suspect when, after a passage of weeks, he admits to Landrum that he did enter the empty store where the child said she had seen him. He has no satisfactory explanation for his failure to tell the truth in the first place. Where, then, is the hope of mankind if a highly educated man, who relies on scientific reason and objectivity in the normal course of life, can be the victim of submerged emotions? Miss Smith's message is that the prospects for rational behavior among average citizens are remote.

One small ray of optimism to be found in *One Hour* lies in the author's view that sexual matters should be freely discussed for better understanding and improvement in human behavior. Thus a minor theme, as evidenced by the minister-spokesman, is that sex, in all its variety, is not sinful. When the notion of sin is eradicated, the implication is that the various taboos surrounding sex can be dissipated; and men and women will then be emotionally free. Presumably, emotional freedom will result in understanding and tolerance, which will lead to rational human behavior. The millennium is not here, however; and *One Hour* embodies one squalid catastrophe after another, ending finally with a Ku Klux Klan cross-burning and murder.

Even the Reverend Landrum, as liberated as he is supposed to be, is not able to perform his duties without prejudice or to behave without suffering guilt. He analyzes his own motives and rationalizes his behavior without apparent self-improvement. And the reader is somewhat shocked by all that is implied in the portrayal of Landrum, as well as Tracy Deen, as cripples. Despite the fact that they have sexual affairs, they are both sexually impaired: Deen is able to have an affair only with a woman whom he and society consider to be his inferior; Landrum, only with a woman who is married to another man. Neither is capable of achieving a satisfactory marital relationship. The scene in which Landrum seduces Grace Channing, not long after the death of Grace's son, is remarkable for its psychological implications. Landrum describes one part of the bed scene as follows: " . . . we were hurting but we could laugh; and she kissed me again and I kissed her and then she put her breast on my mouth and then slowly slowly this woman who had years ago given me back my confidence as a person, gave me not what I had lost—how could she? or anyone?—but something I had never had and never known." Thus, at best, man is immature and psychologically impaired. Until such time as he can overcome these imperfections, there is little hope, either for understanding in interpersonal relationships or for humane and rational self-government.

IV *Style*

Miss Smith's discursive style, seemingly appropriate for her purposes, was not wholly successful for two reasons: (1) the use of the first-person narrator, Reverend Landrum, as a significant character in the novel and as the voice of the author, led Miss Smith into excessive ramblings and posturing; and (2) her constant concern with her moral purpose caused her to make her points repeatedly, leaving nothing to the intellect or imagination of the reader.

On the other hand, Miss Smith did not have the difficulties in using the language that had plagued some of her Naturalistic predecessors, notably Frank Norris and Theodore Dreiser. She could say eloquently and specifically what she wanted to say. It was her teacher-preacher method of engulfing her audience that weakened *One Hour*. As evidenced by her nonfiction writings, Miss Smith believed that man was in control of his own evolution and that, in order to evolve further upon the scale of humanity, he must get busy and change his ways. Here was an honorable moral point, and she undertook to do her part toward the perfection of man by holding a mirror up to him. If she went too far in the enumeration of human flaws and in the volume of correctives she offered, her effort must be acknowledged as timely, sincere, and provocative.

V *Criticism*

While *One Hour* makes interesting reading, it is not so successful, as a work of art, as *Strange Fruit*. Edmund Fuller called attention to some of the flaws that marred the novel at the time of its publication:

> Powerful material is latent in the situation. The control of its force requires focus, discipline, compression, and understatement. Miss Smith, instead, resorted to diffusion and excessive emotionalism, though the latter is not vulgarly obvious.
> She has packed in so much that she clutters up her study of the causes and effects of such an event.[3]

Fuller, who thought the book was "psychoanalyzed to death," finally concluded: "Miss Smith's effort to encompass all the sins and sorrows of man, to create a microcosm to end all microcosms, to be liberal, just, righteous, and realistic, to be a social caseworker, spiritual counselor, and clinical psychologist, all at once, falls by the weight of its over-elaboration."[4]

Although the complaints that the novel was too long were valid, Paul West also touched on aspects of the novel that troubled other reviewers:

> *One hour* is swollen with the often inconsequential reveries of the narrator, David Landrum, Rector of All Saints, Windsor Hills, a town in Virginia. He realizes that he, no less than an unreasoning mob, sees what he wants to see; that is the book's theme. But to my mind, Miss Smith's decision to exemplify that theme in the narrator blurs the action needlessly. . . . Massive themes, grouped like monoliths, cast shadows through the decent-seeming town and the narrator's mind. I find this a difficult, foggy but profound and stunningly fluent piece of writing; the last 100 pages are nerve-wracking. But I'd prefer that clergyman as just another character, with less to say, and less about those philosophy books they all seem to be devouring as dumbly as rabbits.[5]

Another review concluded: "A thick, earnest novel about a nasty affair. . . . Miss Smith, alas, is too meditative for her story; although she piles sorrows on horrors, she muses away all the excitement."[6]

The flaws cited by Fuller and others derive from a structural failure in *One Hour*. Ordinarily, the first-person narrator serves as a controlling and unifying force for the authorial material. In her desire to write the comprehensive novel, however, Miss Smith seemed unable to concentrate upon one central action throughout the book. The role of the narrator, Reverend Landrum, shifts in the course of the novel, with the result that the focus shifts. In the beginning, the novel is *about* Dr. Channing and what happened to him in Windsor Hills, with the narrator serving as a minor character and as an intellectual observer of what takes place. Eventually, the focus shifts to the community where the emphasis is upon the strange behavior of individuals from janitors to senators and the story seems to be *about* the subconscious motivations of all human beings, with the narrator serving as analyst. With a third shift in focus, from the outside world to the inner concerns of the narrator, the novel appears to be *about* Landrum, the modern priest who cannot seem to establish a self-respecting role for himself. In this final stage, Landrum becomes the center of his own narration, repeatedly analyzing himself in such meditations as the following:

> As a priest I had not found the spiritual courage, or was it the desire, to do what I had to do—there was another way for me and I had not found it . . . things to say and I had not said them . . . warnings to give and I had not given them . . . renunciations to make and I had not made them . . . always between me and the irrevocable commitment was the good guy: *me*, the good guy who didn't like to offend his friends, didn't like to stir up disunity in his congregation, didn't like to look at evil when it came too close—never wholly accepting the lonely stark uncharted mission that was mine.

Thus, *One Hour* embodies sufficient material for at least three novels; and, despite the first-person narrator, the work is not unified.

After the publication of *One Hour*, Miss Smith's exploration of the thought and behavior of human beings became more and more personal. In various nonfiction works, she revealed her own thought and observations regarding man's purpose in the universe.

CHAPTER 5

The Non-fiction Writer

I *The Columnist*

T HE bulk of Lillian Smith's writing falls under the heading of nonfiction. She was a writer with several messages to convey, and the quickest and most direct way for her to make her points was through newspaper columns, magazine articles, book reviews, and nonfiction books. In 1948-49, she wrote a series of forty-three weekly columns for the *Chicago Defender*.[1] The heading of her column was "A Southerner Talking," and at the bottom of each article in large letters was the legend "Adventures in Race Relations." Her most frequent themes in these articles had to do with life in the South, the "sickness" of the South, the innocence of children, segregation, sin, politics, religion, world suffering, communism, China, books, art, motion pictures, the wholeness of mankind, Americans for Democratic Action, lynching, and Southern liberals.

Miss Smith was deeply affected by her early life in a rigid, religion-centered home environment and in a segregated community. To the extent that she used her writings to explore every facet of her own experience and feelings, her nonfiction works amount to a continuation of her fictional ones. In her first column for the *Chicago Defender*, she gave a word picture of the mountain on which she was living and reminisced about her childhood in the South. "There were good things in that childhood; good sweet things; mixed up with the bitter poison of White Supremacy and the awful poverty of so much of our region. And those of us born there, unless hurt too much, still love the sweet and the good, though we fear more and more the poison."

In the same column she discussed the recent election of Herman Talmadge as governor of Georgia, saying that his election only meant that the "confusion has deepened." She frequently spoke of the South and Southerners as being confused. She expressed her belief that many Georgians, particularly church women, who were liberals in matters of race might have voted for Talmadge's opponent but voted instead for Talmadge because they believed "liquor" to be the real moral issue and "race" the political issue. Again she wrote, "minds are confused, people are worried, many hearts are frightened, but the South is changing."

Miss Smith maintained her own hopeful, somewhat mystical, dreamlike vision of what human life should and could be like. In her second column, she ruminated upon hog-killing in Georgia, which had to occur when the moon is right; and then she led into the moral point she wished to make:

> Sometimes it seems to me that a terrible illness has us in its clutches, driving us to set up mad, impossible barriers of color, of wealth, of religion, of "belief," even of sex, separating us one from the other, and making us hate and fear and want to destroy in the name of Utter Foolishness so much that is sweet and good and wonderful. It is like a nightmare. I wish we could wake up, stretch our hearts and minds and spirits and smile at each other and say, "Good morning, everybody. This is a fine day for fun and living, isn't it?" And hear the whole world answer, "Yes, it's a fine day for fun and living—and the moon is just right."

In one column, which she wrote in her library on the mountain, she recalled various people who had visited in that room. Since her home and library were part of the summer camp for girls which she had operated for many years, she naturally had memories of the many children who had been there. From time to time, as in this column and other works, Miss Smith showed a startling capacity for going from vicious criticism to a rather unconvincing tolerance of persons and situations. Although the Talmadges, Herman and his father, Gene, were among the Southerners she disliked most, she wrote in this column that, "While 'Gene' Talmadge was never here, most of his friends have been here and many have sent their children to my camp. How strange is this world we live in! How wrong it is to stereotype people as all 'good' or all 'bad'; how hard it is to remember that there is a human being in each of us if we can but find him."

In December, 1948, she wrote a long column on China and communism. She acknowledged that the Communists seemed to be winning China, and she wrote: "We cannot let the communists take over there but we cannot let the Chiangs continue their gigantic failure. They seem to me not only to have failed morally but they have failed as strategists. The Chiangs are not good enough for

China. Somehow new leadership must be found." She commented upon the inherent dignity of the Chinese people, their respect for the individual, and then she said that she had felt strange, years ago, coming from "the South where human dignity is held so cheap" to live in China where each individual is precious. She learned while in China, she said, that "segregation is a lynching of the personality and worse than physical lynching."

As she discussed some of the failures of the white man in China, she included the fact that British and Americans had "Jim Crowed the pleasantest spots in Shanghai" when she was there. Yet she had hope for China: "I know that in the long run totalitarianism hasn't a chance in China." To her, as to many others, it seemed that,

> In the long run, the Chinese would merely turn communism to their own uses. The danger now is that they will accept it temporarily, under stress, and this acceptance will open wide the door to its acceptance in India and throughout Asia. The earth is in such a delicate equilibrium that one door swinging open, swings a dozen more wide open. The real problem is that all eyes are on communism. If we could make democracy as interesting, if we could make the world turn and look at us and keep looking because they liked what they saw, problems that now seem near insoluble would simply fade into nothing.

In August, 1949, Miss Smith commented upon the news about Paul Robeson and his wife and their Communist affiliations. She had met them in New York during the Broadway production of *Strange Fruit*; in fact, Robeson had been one of the few prominent Negroes in the country to praise Miss Smith's play. As she recalled the incident, he came backstage and congratulated the cast with tears in his eyes. Although she was always strongly anti-Communist, Lillian Smith's sympathy for the Negro in white societies gave her some understanding of the predicament of the Negro who was earnestly trying to find his place in the world. She regretted that communism sometimes appeared to be the only way out:

> I have been troubled by things I have read in the papers lately about the Robesons. I know them both and like them. I cannot believe we are getting the whole story; certainly we are not getting it in all of its complexity. All I can say here is that I wish the white press would stop heckling them. I cannot see how any white person who has a grain of sportsmanship in him can criticize any Negro, who, in confusion, has turned to communism for the answer that democracy has not yet given. Com-

munism is a poor answer as I say again and again but we white folks have not yet given Negroes in the South a better one. Until we do, I wish we had the grace to keep our mouths shut.

In regard to racism, there were frequent references to mental illness, a subject in which she had a lifelong interest, in her columns for the *Defender*. Miss Smith was concerned with the individual's mental problems on a national scale; but she was convinced, though she was not wholly convincing on the subject, that most Southerners were mentally ill because of an obsession with racism.

About the racial situation in the South, however, she sometimes seemed to be more optimistic than current events and situations warranted. For instance, on June 18, 1949, she predicted that in five years there would be almost no *legal* segregation left in the South, a prediction which did not come true until July 2, 1964, with the passage of the Federal Civil Rights Law. In the same column she wrote: "I do not believe hate can be legislated out or mental health legislated in but I think laws can be taken off books that now make legal the many actions that injure people's physical and mental health." In spite of the fact that President Truman's Civil Rights Bill was being shunted aside by Congress at the time she was writing, Miss Smith was optimistic about the future of race relations in the South: "In spite of the fact that the sick patient still has temperature, there are signs that he is going to get well."

On another occasion she began her column by discussing the various fevers which were prevalent, causing widespread illness and death, during her childhood; then she moved to the subject of the mental health of residents of the South: "Today, minds and hearts of southern people are swept by worse fevers. Our health as people is endangered even more than in the old days. But we have not worked out sewage systems to take off hate and fear that now are epidemic; nor have we cleaned up the contaminated spots in our culture; nor have we got rid of the carriers of hate and fear, nor have we inoculated our people with beliefs in human dignity and freedom that can stop the growth of these feelings in our minds."

A few weeks later, in a candid moment, Miss Smith voiced her awareness that at least some people were not being moved by what she and others were doing and saying: "The St. Louis and Washington riots, as well as the violence of the Klan in the South make us know that there is a vast multitude of white people who are not being touched by our books, articles and projects in human relations."

As she had done and was to do on numerous occasions, she expressed her belief that white supremacy was largely responsible for the spread of communism in the world and for most of the problems which the Western democracies have faced in this century. With regard to communism in China, she said, "Every wise person saw this thing coming twenty years ago. I knew when I was there that this would happen if we did not change our ways." After asking "Why were we so blind?" she wrote: "I do not know. But I know today that without a big moral gesture made by us we cannot keep the Orient from accepting Communism. We can save the rest of the Far East only by laying down white supremacy as a way of life. Are we strong enough to do it? brave enough? honest enough? wise enough? I do not know."

Mrs. Eleanor Roosevelt was the person Lillian Smith most admired. Miss Smith responded strongly on August 27, 1949. to Cardinal Spellman's attack on Mrs. Roosevelt. She said that, although the attack had been squelched in the press, Cardinal Spellman had made millions of people realize that Mrs. Roosevelt was the "most deeply respected" person in the world. She called her a symbol of all that is good for mankind, such as freedom, peace, and dignity. She placed Mrs. Roosevelt above Queen Bess of England, Madame Chiang Kai-shek, Helen of Troy, and Joan of Arc, and "other women who have fought for their own and others' rights."

Mrs. Roosevelt, Miss Smith thought, stood for the world of the future: "There are a lot of people who are against this future. They want to return to the past, and to their version of it. They cannot accept the awful fact that the past has ended. When will White Supremacy see it, when will Communism see it, when will the Church see it? When will the old powers confess that all authority is doomed, all arrogance, all power to enslave the individual's body and mind and soul?" In her New Year's column, Miss Smith made a long list of wishes that covered literally everybody in the world, including her idol: "For Mrs. Roosevelt, many years of good health and more and more mileage; for each mile Our Lady travels is one more mile in her network of goodwill."

Senator Paul Douglas and the then Senator Hubert Humphrey were also greatly admired by Miss Smith, but Senator Douglas lost some favor with her when she concluded from certain statements he had made that he was making a compromise with the South on matters of civil rights:

> The old familiar phrase: "We are not proposing to abolish segregation in the South; we just want—" sounds evil enough at home in Georgia, but when said with a Yankee accent it makes one feel sick all over.

> I am sorry that Paul Douglas felt he must say it. I am a bit more than sorry; I am shocked that he felt he must stoop to a double-talk that fools no Southerner.

Occasionally, Miss Smith's personal anxiety was revealed in her writings. In the course of relating an episode involving a mad dog, she wrote: "Mad dog . . . racing down the quiet road where children play. That is the way of life. Never are we sure that we are peaceful and serene and safe. Always danger lurks, waiting to creep on us in our most tranquil moment." Her agressive concern for the mental and physical well-being of every human being on earth and her determined search for someone to blame for human imperfections may also indicate a deep-seated, vaguely defined personal anxiety. She tended to blame preachers, Southern liberals, white supremacists, chivalry, weak mothers, newspaper editors, and poor whites at one time or another for segregation. Everybody was to blame for the lack of understanding of mentally disturbed and physically handicapped people. When Miss Smith thought a situation needed correcting, she called for immediate action without compromise. She never agreed with Flannery O'Connor's view, which Stanley E. Hyman has summed up as follows: "Miss O'Connor insists with Dostoevski that the only equality is to be found in the spiritual dignity of man, in the mystic communion of the Sacraments."[2]

Because of Miss Smith's militant approach to problems of racial segregation, she had little admiration for Hodding Carter, Ralph McGill, and other Southern liberals who took a more moderate view. She thought they could have been more effective against Governor Herman Talmadge and others:

> As long as we have the sore of segregation we are going to have a foul drainage from it. If the drainage is heavy enough, repulsive enough, maybe southern liberals will finally see that there can be no health in Dixie as long as segregation is there. Maybe men like Hodding

The Non-fiction Writer

Carter, Ralph McGill, Jack Tarver, Wright Bryan will finally learn
to fight the causes of our trouble and waste less drama on the symptoms.

★ ★ ★

When will our newspaper editors and columnists and our preachers
learn to look at the sore? When will they finally confess that all this
drainage befouling the South, infecting its children, is oozing out of the
sore? When will they finally understand that the sore itself springs from
a virulent idea with which the white man is infected, and this idea of
white superiority has taken hold of him because of sickness already
in his home and culture?

In one column, Miss Smith said, "When I have become weighed
down with the world's misery I go to the kitchen and cook." But she
did not understand how thoughtful people could enjoy food with
millions of hungry children in the world. Sending a check to CARE
would help the conscience, she thought. Then she referred to her
own burden:

> Sometimes the burden of the world's misery is almost too heavy to
> bear when there are so few people bearing it. One wonders how long
> we can keep at it without losing our humor, our balance, our tender
> concern for our own personal relationships; and more than all else,
> how we can feel compassion for the very ones whose sins are destroying
> our earth's children. It is so easy to hate; it is so much harder to under-
> stand. Yet only understanding can rid the world of the EVILS WHICH
> MAKE YOU AND ME EVIL, and the "others" evil also.

Again she saw the world's problem as two-pronged: "We have two
big jobs today: one to make our world whole by healing the splits
between people; the other is to make ourselves whole by healing
the splits within our own minds and hearts." The problem, to
Lillian Smith is that people simply will not quit doing what they are
doing to each other. Children are innocent in her moral scheme,
but they fall from grace as they grow into men and women, not
because of any defect within themselves but because of the influence of their parents and of society upon them.

Her concern for the trials of children is evident in her comments
upon *The Quiet One*, a motion picture which was set in Harlem:
"A camera in the hands of one sensitive to the light and darkness
and movement of a child's soul can do powerful things to an adult's
peace of mind. There were moments when I found the film almost

79

unendurable, so ruthless was its exposure of our civilization's cruelties to children." She contended that the setting could have been Park Avenue or North Atlanta since "it hurts as much to be rejected by a rich mother as by a poor one. We watch the youngster as he is so nearly destroyed as a human being and we see him begin to grow again." She praised the film's music which had been composed by Ulysses Kay, and she said that James Agee had "written a sensitive commentary" on the production.

When she wrote about having studied Picasso's works over a period of several months, she admittedly thought him highly skilled; but she was sickened by the total effect of his work. She posed her reasons for disappointment with contemporary artists in the form of a question: "Are artists so chained to our age that they, too, cannot see things whole, they, too, are unable to affirm life and love and sorrow and laughter and tenderness?" After visiting an exhibition of American artists at the Downtown Gallery, she said: "American painters when they do not abjectly imitate the French schools cannot rid themselves of their natural gusto, their roving eye, their adolescent brag and daring and their laughter and tenderness. It gets in the paint somehow, even when they are trying hard to be decadent."

II *The Essayist*

Miss Smith terminated her column in the *Chicago Defender* in the fall of 1949 in order to devote more time to the writing of books and articles. She was also in demand as a speaker, and her prepared speeches often found their way into print. After the notoriety of *Strange Fruit*, she remained for the general public that unusual person: a Southern white woman who wrote and spoke against segregation and who did not hesitate to criticize those whom she thought were responsible for the South's predicament. Although she was more rewarded and remembered for her objections to racial segregation, she was deeply concerned with various personal, national, and international problems. A selecion of her articles and speeches illustrate the manner in which Miss Smith accepted her responsibility, as she saw it, to speak out regarding her region and her world.

In September, 1944, long before she had spoken of segregation as "a lynching of the personality" in the *Chicago Defender*, she wrote for the *New Republic* an article "Addressed to White

Liberals" in which she said that segregation constituted "Spiritual lynching."[3] In this article, Miss Smith called for those concerned persons, particularly American liberals, to quit talking about the "Negro problem" and to begin to think and talk of the white man's problem. She called attention to the fact that segregation was not simply a part of the Southern tradition, but that it was "an ancient psychological mechanism used by men the world over whenever they want to shut themselves away from problems which they fear and do not feel they have the strength to solve." She referred to segregation as "cultural schizophrenia":

> It is chilling to note the paranoid symptoms of those among us who cling to segregation: their violence, their sensitiveness to criticism, their stereotyped defenses, their inability to identify their overesteem of themselves with the emotional needs of others, their reluctance to reach out and accept new ideas, their profound desire to withdraw from everything hard to face, everything that requires of their personalities further growth.

> Those who believe in this philosophy of segregation have chosen the schizophrenic way: withdrawing from reality; and this withdrawal has profoundly affected their minds and emotions.

Miss Smith maintained that the interracial problems of the United States were not limited to economic and educational areas; the white race, she said, had used the Negro to vent its own frustrations. She thought that white people should probe themselves to find why they needed segregation. What she suggested sounded rather like a mass psychoanalysis for white Southerners, a suggestion too vague and impractical for most people to accept or undertake. Certainly the individual reader could not glean a practical course of action from this particular article. If indeed the problem is mass mental illness among the white citizens of the United States, Miss Smith, in the role of the doctor, may have spoiled her chances of arresting or healing the illness by shouting at the patient. As a rule, psychiatrists do not give their patients face-to-face diagnoses; they find it better practice to lead their patients in such a way that they gain insight into their own conditions and their causes.

Although she chastised white liberals for contending that segregation must "change slowly," she should have recognized that a mental rearrangement of millions of people, which Miss Smith definitely thought was necessary, would require a substantial span of time.

She offered, however, one practical step for anybody who opposed segregation. She felt that the "conspiracy of silence" should be broken by those who believed in racial integration; they should make their voices heard, just as the racists were doing. And, in the course of her address to white liberals, Miss Smith took up one of her favorite subjects: children in a segregated society. She thought that white supremacy bred arrogance in white children and that it restricted the growth and personality development of Negro children. She believed that segregation created something less than human out of little children, causing them to lynch and be lynched.

In a later issue of the *New Republic*, Edmund Rucker, a native Southerner then living in California, wrote a letter to the editor in which he called attention to the weaknesses in Miss Smith's article. He wondered what individuals could do about racial problems. In asking for a course of action, he wrote: "I twice read Lillian Smith's lamentation on the Negro's wrongs without discovering any clue as to what she thinks can be done to change the attitude of whites—which is the real and unsurmountable barrier—or what she herself is doing about it."[4] Miss Smith's response to Rucker's letter was published in the same issue with his under the heading "How to Work for Racial Equality."[5]

She offered three answers which can be summarized as follows:

(1) White people should look into the matter of the white man's need to feel superior, and they should try to realize that segregation damages white children.

(2) "Racial hate and prejudice have dug deep chasms. These chasms can be filled only by each individual going to the edge of them and dumping into those terrifying depths his personal need to hate." She also thought that Negroes too might have to do some "dumping."

(3) The chasms could be bridged by cooperation among people, who should work for laws against segregation and for state and national Fair Employment Practices Committees; work to remove the poll tax and the white primary in the South; try to move toward justice in the courts; work to increase employment, including federal projects; work for federal aid to education; make friends with people of other races through interracial organizations; sit with and communicate with Negroes when the opportunity occurs; and refrain

from telling race jokes and commend people who are working in the cause of good race relations.

Miss Smith, who obviously resented Mr. Rucker's comment on her essay, called him "querulous" and referred to his letter as "fretful and nervous." But Mr. Rucker had a point in that Miss Smith's abstract idealism regarding how things *ought* to be did not offer many practical answers as to how change can be effected. She refused to say specifically what she did to bring about change, saying that Mr. Rucker would not ask her to do that if he understood what it was to be on the "firing line" day and night. If he understood that, she said, "he would no more ask me to advertise what I do and what I don't do than he would ask General MacArthur to disclose his next week's strategy." It must be admitted, however, that Miss Smith's vagueness regarding a program for mental health or other changes in a segregated culture reduced the effectiveness of her writings over a thirty-year period. The average person finds it difficult to visualize the process of dumping a bucketful of hate into an invisible chasm.

In a speech which she gave in Arkansas in 1956, later published in the *New Republic* as "No Easy Way, Now,"[6] she discussed mobs, saying that the mob is made up of a handful of people. She questioned how so few people could be successful; and she answered her own question by blaming the men in the offices—bankers, doctors, clerks—for silently protecting the mob when it went into action; and such silent onlookers formed one kind of mob. She also thought there must be another kind of mob "which lives in the depths of every man's mind: It is activated by primitive fears, hatreds, guilts, some of which have nothing whatever to do with race. It is nourished on anxiety about the body image, on anxiety about our personal relationships, and on the terrors that arise like a miasma from ancient myths of birth, death, blood, heredity, animals, darkness." She went on to say that this mob "makes its home on the prehistoric, mythic level of the human mind. We are born possessing this symbolizing layer of mind—and everybody in the South seems to have an extra amount of it! It is a pity that reason is not born in us."

As in the above explanation of the source of the mob instinct in man, Miss Smith sometimes seemed to be saying that there is no plausible way to change man's attitudes for the improvement of society. On other occasions, of course, she indicated that the social milieu created the problems in race relations and that they could be changed. Miss Smith mentioned in the Arkansas speech other barriers to the improvements of race relations:

> There are . . . hundreds of gifted, articulate white southerners ready to speak to the entire nation— and across the magnolia curtain to their South—but where can they do it? National magazines with mass circulation don't want articles from white southerners who oppose segregation; they want articles from the "moderates" and from the separate-but-equalers, and the gradualists, and from the Faulkners who say, "Give up folks; there's nothing to do; whites and Negroes just don't like each other, etc." (This is Mr. Faulkner's mythic mind speaking: the only mind he has ever really shown evidence of possessing; for not much critical intelligence is in his novels; only his mythic gift shows: it is rich, it is wonderful; but it, alone, does not make great literature, nor great art, nor great leadership.)

She also charged that television and radio networks were not offering white Southerners the opportunity to oppose segregation, saying that she had appeared on a national program once, only for a moment. She complained that segregationalists, such as "Talmadge and Eastland," and certain "muted moderates," appeared on national programs frequently. By 1965 Miss Smith had lost faith in some of the Northern liberals who had fallen, she said, for "the line" of the Southern moderates and even the credo of the White Citizens Councils.

In an effort to point the way for well-meaning citizens, she cited several things that must be done by those who could and would take up the task. She thought that the American people had to be convinced that national survival depended upon the willingness to accord citizenship rights to Negroes, that the moral and spiritual good of the people depended upon such recognition, that mob rule should be put down, and that the fear of intermarriage should be cleared from "the caves of our minds." Then she again criticized the Southern moderate: "But there should be no room down here for the hater, the bigot. My strongest objection to the self-named 'moderate' is their quite awful bigotry. Their intolerance of us who work perhaps with more non-violence but with more candor, too, would be an incredible thing, were it not so human."

In "The Mob and the Ghost," first published in 1962, Miss Smith asserted that in her opinion "mobs and demagogues, riots and hate slogans," indicated a "collective illness." She wrote:

The South is suffering from such a malaise. The illness is by no means limited to the South or to our country. It comes not primarily from racism (racism is a symptom, not the disease itself); it comes from two centuries of Western man's misunderstanding of science and over-esteem of proof and from his unnecessary subjection to the machine he created. Combined, these have caused him to misinterpret religion, have pushed him toward the facts of the laboratory and away from the truth found in poetry. And now, most men no longer believe that there is something bigger than a man, that spiritual laws exist which no one can disregard without destroying himself.[7]

Although she never confessed any strong religious beliefs, Lillian Smith frequently used the word "sin" with regard to racial segregation and other human acts. Although Miss Smith was reared in a rigidly Methodist family, her reader is never quite sure whether she is talking about sin as it is defined in the Methodist credo or whether she has some secular definition for the word. In the above article, for instance, she wrote: "Of all our Southern sins—and we have plenty—the persistent, blind ignoring of the needs of our poor and ignorant whites is perhaps the worst; our culture has fed them lies—not folk wisdom; our power structure, instead of giving jobs, gave them for decades a false and ridiculous sense of superiority, teaching them that excellence lay simply in possessing white skin."

As time passed, Miss Smith abandoned the hope that religionists, politicians, and scientists would solve the problems of race relations. She came more and more to believe that only the poet could save mankind. In "The Mob and the Ghost," she discussed the idea that demagogues assume the authority of priests in telling gullible people what they are justified in doing and that the people believe them. Once the violence was released, she said, only physical force could control the evil doings of the demagogue; but the inner turmoil of man could be controlled only by poetic truth. She said:

The poet, therefore, is the demagogue's mortal enemy—for he and he alone can overcome the evil state of men's minds. The poet can do this not only because he, too, uses ghosts—"the good ghosts"—but because he has power over the poetic truth-seeking levels of the mythic mind. This is why the silence of the poet in all of us is so dread a thing when the mob begins to merge. This is the moment when only truth can kill the lie, when only love can weaken hate; reason cannot do it, nor common sense, nor logic; but poetic truth spoken to people with compassion and beauty has the strange power to arouse their good feelings and desires.

The mythic mind is, above all else, highly creative: it can create lies and demons and mobs and riots; but it can also create art and poetry by careful addition of heart and intelligence and the proper use of symbols and ghosts. What the demagogues do is to change gold into straw; what the poets do is to change straw into gold.

Several years later, writing in the *Saturday Review*, Miss Smith restated the idea that poets, not scientists or statesmen, must lead mankind out of the modern chaos.[8] Exactly how the poet could accomplish this, when the influence of poets and literary artists of all kinds appeared to be waning, Miss Smith did not explain. Something in her mystical turn of mind, which had been evolving over a period of years, culminated in the idea that only poetry was free of the taint of racial prejudice. Her high confidence that psychoanalysis could heal the patient of his disease of racial prejudice suffered a serious decline when she concluded that man might never be able to use reason to overcome emotion. She came more and more to believe in some spiritual insight more effective than organized religion to lift man from the mire of subhuman behavior. In the last-mentioned essay, she discussed the audience upon which demagogues must rely, saying that these people are "ignorant" and "culturally stunted." Regarding mob action, she said, "The strain of living in both a spiritual vacuum and a scientific world which is totally beyond their comprehension is eased by this frank regression to more primitive ways."

On November 19, 1954, Lillian Smith delivered a Sidney Hillman Lecture at Roosevelt University with the title, "Demagoguery: World-Size Danger. Have We World-Size Defenses?" She began by wondering what there was in communism which appealed to Asians and what there was in democracy which did not appeal to them. The answer, she said, could be found in two words, *poverty* and *color*. The kind of poverty she had observed in China and India, she said, had never been experienced in the United States although its poverty was bad enough and too prevalent for comfort.

The colonial powers had not caused the poverty and ignorance in Asia, but Miss Smith thought that they could have done more to alleviate them during the long years when they had had power there. She cited instances of British cruelty in India when the natives protested British rule and of segregation of the races throughout Asia by whites prior to the Communist success in China. She felt that the Communists had taken complete advantage of the failures of Western powers by promising Asians relief from poverty and racial segregation. As for the Asian people, "They have had enough of 'white democracy.' They are, to put it bluntly, fed up. Communist colonialism may be ten times worse than the brand of colonialism they have experienced for two centuries—but, at least, it is something different."

In the second half of her lecture, Miss Smith discussed what she regarded as defenses against demagoguery in the United States. The rule of law she placed as the first defense. In spite of Senator Joseph McCarthy and Southern demagogues, she contended that, as long as Americans respect the decisions of the Supreme Court and believe in the Constitution and Bill of Rights, citizens of the United States have a first line of defense against dictatorship. She argued for a stronger United Nations through which the rule of law might be extended to the whole world.

A second line of defense lay in courageous, intelligent leadership: "A good leader speaks out more plainly than demagogues speak. He also understands the human heart and knows how to talk its language. He must be as good a psychologist as is the demagogue. He must be warm. He must feel deeply about fundamentals, human experiences. Demagogues are not afraid of feeling deeply about things"; indeed, demagogues manipulate peoples' feelings for their own purposes. And some otherwise fine leaders have failed because they did not trust their feelings and placed intellect above feeling. Woodrow Wilson, she believed, had failed in this country because he could not empathize with the people. Although she did not name a person whom she considered to be a good leader, she said that preachers, teachers, politicians, almost anybody might, with courage, become true leaders.

A third defense against demagoguery involved education against the tactics of the demagogue. This education should begin in elementary school, but television could offer a quick way to reach the general public. Miss Smith thought that the television exposé of Joseph McCarthy had taught the American people a great deal about demagoguery. Moreover, education should be more positive in helping the American people to understand better their own democracy. This study of the meaning of democracy should begin in the public schools and continue into adulthood.

Miss Smith then said that definitely and specifically the American people could defend themselves against "demagoguery . . . , Communist or home-grown variety," by putting an end to segregation. She thought the United States would gain stature in the eyes of Asian and African countries by integration of the races; at the same time, it could defeat one of the strongest arguments of the Communists in those countries. She also thought that the Asian people would like Americans better if the United States would lend money to them for improvement projects rather than make charitable grants in Asian countries. She spoke particularly of the mutual benefits to be derived from lending money to India for industrial development, the results of which would be increased trade between India and the United States.

In this lecture, as on many other occasions, Miss Smith revealed herself to be more adept at spotting and discussing the problems of demagoguery than at outlining solutions. She spoke feelingly against some of the failings of the American people and the short-comings of the American democracy, but she had not given sufficient thought to finding any original ideas for resolving these matters. Her suggestions regarding education and economic aid, which had been projected by numerous national figures, were already familiar to her listeners.

Some months after the enforced school integration in New Orleans, Lillian Smith went to that city and talked with various women about their attitudes on segregation. As a result, her article "The Ordeal of Southern Women" was published in *Redbook*.[9] She found some of the women tormented by their doubts about segregation, but even those who were convinced that it was right to integrate the schools were helpless within the political and social structure. For this article, Miss Smith received the Sidney Hillman Award for the best magazine writing in 1961. She was too ill to appear in person to receive the award, but her written response was later published in *Redbook* under the heading, "An Awakening of the Heart."

In her acceptance speech, she wrote about the courage of the people she encountered in the cobalt room of the cancer center, then she said: "As I turn from the cobalt room to my own South, I realize that the only enemies we Southerners have are ourselves. The Yankees are not against us; the United Nations is not against us (as the John Birchers claim); even Russia is not our Number One enemy. But anxiety, and ignorance and greed—and above all else, a curious moral blindness that breeds complacency." [10]

She repeated some of her experiences in New Orleans which had appeared in the article for which she received the award. Then she spoke of herself: "As a writer, my special point of view, my personal way of looking at life, has been determined by my experiences with segregation—which is far more than a social or economic or political problem. Segregation is a symptom of a de-humanized way of life that springs from our loss of vision of the human being and the future." [11]

On January 14, 1966, a long letter to the editor from Lillian Smith was published in the *Atlanta Constitution* regarding the exclusion of Julian Bond from the Georgia legislature. Julian Bond, a young Negro and one of the leaders of the Student Non-Violent Coordi-nating Committee, had been elected to the legislature; but the legislators had refused him his seat because he objected to the war in Vietnam and had expressed sympathy for young men who burned their draft cards. In Miss Smith's letter, reprinted as an article in *New South* with the title "Miss Smith on SNCC,"[12] she said that she had been shocked when the leadership of this organization had called for the burning of draft cards; but, after thinking over the matter, she was reminded of the problems of Selma and of the murder of her personal friend, the Unitarian minister James Reeb. She thought, too, of the many ways in which Georgians had disre-garded the Constitution of the United States in their treatment of the Negro people, but she regarded their legislators as suddenly and dramatically pious with regard to the Constitution: "What right have they—of all people!—to decide they could judge Bond's belief in democracy when for much of their lifetime they've done all they could to keep us from ever living a real democracy in the South?"

Miss Smith took this opportunity to tell the world why she had not opposed President Johnson's handling of the war in Vietnam. Because she had lived in China and spent time in India and had studied Asian matters for some years, she recognized the complexity of Asian matters: "I wish the war could stop today; I wish we could begin to negotiate tomorrow but, as I wrote a well-known Harvard professor who rather angrily accused me of becoming 'a little reactionary,' I simply know too much about it to take the simplistic position (and the highly angered and discourteous position) that so many of my friends in the North have taken."

She acknowledged that the United States had made errors with regard to China, errors which went all the way back to the failure to aid Sun Yat-sen in 1923-24 and which included the mistake of accepting Chiang and Formosa as the true China and not permitting China in the United Nations. She said that mistakes on China had been made by Presidents Harding, Coolidge, Truman, Eisenhower, and Kennedy, but "the leftists, even some of my friends, who I had thought about as moderately liberal, have turned angrily against Johnson insisting like children that we do something he simply cannot do. Hating him (and Rusk) largely because they are southern (I find myself thinking this)."

Apparently, considerable pressure had been put upon Miss Smith to sign various statements against the Vietnam war, but she refused to sign "partly because of the rudeness of the language and partly because of the shallowness and simplistic suggestions on what should be done." While she thought Julian Bond naive, she said that she could understand how frustrated young Negroes might accept the advice of Staughton Lynd and others who had come South and infiltrated the movement for civil rights. She said that white Southerners, their newspapers and legislators, would walk into a trap if they undertook to punish a few misguided people. Julian Bond, she thought, should have the "right to be wrong."

Finally Miss Smith ended her letter by expressing her respect for the President: "I am an admirer of Johnson's; I think he is a genius of a man; he has great virtues, also big faults; but this time I think he is earnestly trying to find the right way; and I want us to speak against war, to urge negotiations but to respect his efforts to bring these matters about. Neither SNCC nor the Georgia legislature is helping Johnson bring us closer to peace."

Lillian Smith also had great admiration for the Reverend Dr. Martin Luther King and for his work through the Southern Christian Leadership Conference. Having long been convinced of the merits of the nonviolent approach to social problems because of her observations of Ghandi in India, Miss Smith gave high praise to Dr. King in an article in *Saturday Review* in 1962. [13] She believed it would be a serious mistake for any minority group to adopt the tactics which white men have used against them for centuries. In her view, there had to be a coming together of people—not a widening of the gap between them.

In 1966, after the Congress of Racial Equality followed the leadership of the Student Non-Violent Coordinating Committee in adopting the black-power slogan, Miss Smith resigned her membership in CORE. Although she was seriously ill again with cancer, she was alert to the significance of what the new leaders of CORE and SNCC were doing, and she thought them misguided and doomed to bring about new barriers to racial equality. She was firm in her resignation, but she was not quite so sharp as the Mauldin cartoon in which SNCC and CORE were depicted as little boys in short pants, throwing away the umbrella of nonviolence, with CORE saying, "If it rains, we'll spit back."

III   *The Critic*

Lillian Smith's comments on books by other writers are particularly interesting for what they revealed about her and her taste in literature. During the 1960's, she was a regular reviewer for the *Chicago Tribune Book Review*. Among the books she especially enjoyed reviewing were the recent translations of the works of Teilhard de Chardin, in whom she avowedly found a kindred spirit. The major difference in her view and his, however, lay in the fact that Miss Smith had no such abiding faith as Teilhard's in the ascendancy of Christianity. She did share his compulsive need to reconcile the spiritual life of man with scientific fact and to prove to her own satisfaction that the two could live together. Miss Smith, like Teilhard, was a believer in evolution; and the influence of Teilhard can be detected in her statement to newsman Frank Daniel in 1964:

As an artist I find myself peculiarly sensitive to all that blocks our evolution as human beings. How do we know?—we may be only half way to humanization. In a sense we may have "just begun." There is no telling where mankind can go if we keep facing the future of human evolution.

I cannot but believe that this is the essense of religion: this "getting with" the purpose of the Divine Creator—this refusal ever to turn backward to the things of the past, to conditions less human, less compassionate. . . . I see a persisting purpose in man's existence on this earth.[14]

More than a year later, another interviewer who visited Miss

Smith at her home found her to be optimistic about the future of mankind. Chris Eckl wrote: "One of the foundations for her optimism about the future of man are the writings of the late Pierre Teilhard de Chardin, a Jesuit priest and noted paleontologist, whose books she has reviewed."[15]

As mentioned in the first chapter of this study, Lillian Smith's maternal grandfather had studied to be a Jesuit priest, but he had decided against being a priest and had actually left the Catholic Church. She had, however, a lifelong respect for his intellectuality, a respect which she easily transferred to the person and works of the tortured Teilhard, a Jesuit who undertook to resolve the differences between science and religion so he could remain in the church. Although Teilhard himself seemed satisfied with his synthesis, he expressed dismay and sadness before he died that he was almost alone in seeing the vision which he had created. Since almost nobody seemed to go with him all the way, he even wondered if he might not have been suffering from delusions. During the interim since his death in 1955, Teilhard appears to have gained some stature in the United States as a result of translations of most of his books into English. In reviewing his book, *The Appearance of Man*, Miss Smith wrote: "No writer has written so persuasively, so elegantly (for his words express his style of creative thinking) of man's evolving future; no one can persuade the reluctant skeptic as can Teilhard."[16]

In a review of *Everything That Rises Must Converge* by Flannery O'Connor, Miss Smith naturally noted that the title of the book of stories was taken from the works of Teilhard de Chardin, but it seemed hard for her to believe that Flannery O'Connor, a devout Roman Catholic, might have read Teilhard without agreeing with him. If one were to judge by the fiction and nonfiction writings of Miss O'Connor, he would have to conclude that she had no great optimism about the perfection of man on earth. But, wrote Miss Smith in her review:

Miss O'Connor has read Teilhard de Chardin and, one suspects, with very real enthusiasm; but she seems rather ashamed to be enthusiastic and feels compelled to twist even his profound and poetic vision into something small enough for her to smile at wryly.

She uses his words, "Everything that rises must converge," as the sardonic title of the best story of the collection. In that story Miss

O'Connor has created a masterpiece: every line counts, every word; her tone is right and her vision is multileveled. [17]

Certainly the subject matter of Miss O'Connor's title story—the intrafamily struggles of a segregationist mother and an integrationist son—was congenial to Lillian Smith.

In that same review, she compared Flannery O'Connor's talents to a "cartoonist's drawing," saying they were as limited as a cartoon. In defense of Miss O'Connor, however, it might be pointed out that a cartoon can sometimes say all that needs to be said upon a subject, as in the case of the Bill Mauldin cartoon mentioned above. But, as is well known, Miss Smith liked the big novel, the Naturalistic novel, which gives the causes and the actions and the explanations and which also makes a moral point for change or correction in society. She cited Miss O'Connor's tendency to deal with the kind of reprehensible characters that can be found in the South, but she was impatient with her failure to "write about . . . the blank wall against which these people beat out their lives; nor does she tell us who put the wall up and keeps it there."

Miss Smith then took advantage of the opportunity to express a more general opinion of contemporary literature.

Miss O'Connor does not write of her peers; neither did Faulkner; it is not fashionable, today, to do so. Many sophisticated readers want to read about people who are morally, spiritually and culturally inferior, and many of our most gifted writers (and Miss O'Connor was highly gifted) have responded to that appetite of the cultivated or perhaps it is a phenomenon of our times affecting writer and reader simultaneously. It is curious how quickly a new arrogance can take the place of an outdated one. Racial arrogance now is almost taboo in contemporary writing, but new forms of arrogance (spiritual and cultural) have quickly taken its place.

One can hardly agree with Miss Smith's idea that, of all people, Flannery O'Connor and William Faulkner were deliberately writing in the fashionable manner of their time. For that matter, no writer worth his salt pays obeisance to the "appetite of the cultivated." Miss Smith surely knew, even as she wrote her review, that writers deal with fictional materials in their own way as best they can at any given time.

On another occasion she commented upon the writers of her

region: "All important southern writers of the last three decades have used the deviant as their hero or nonhero; coming out of a conformist One-Idea yet fragmented culture, a totalitarian political pattern of life, swung dizzily by moral polarities, it was inevitable that each in his own way would choose the experiences of Outsiders from which to create the world of his imagination." [18] This quotation is from her review of Oliver Evan's book on Carson McCullers. She panned the book because she thought Mr. Evans lacked the writing skill and imagination to create scenes which would "bring alive Carson McCullers and her amazing family." Miss Smith, of course, knew Carson McCullers and the members of her family personally and in a way that the biographer could not know them.

She never had much patience with Southern writers who were not in the New South tradition. When Daniel asked what she thought about Southern writers, she replied in the *Atlanta Journal* (November 24, 1964):

> What is there to say? I am a good story teller, and there have been others. Perhaps I am more philosophic than most—it is difficult to say. I feel that the present fashion is temporary—it is passing quickly now. We shall soon get back to real things, the meaning of the person, the purpose of our presense on this rather wonderful and terrifying little earth. All this is important.
>
> It is more important than our private sex lives, how we react to this and that. Our old puritanism still holds us to a kind of childlike interest in sex. But we will outgrow much of this, take it more for granted, see that other things are far more important to write about.

In a review of *The Keepers of the House* by Shirley Ann Grau, Miss Smith admitted that the novel had flaws; but she liked it. Miss Grau had, in fact, written exactly the kind of novel Miss Smith admired. Since the novel received the Pulitzer Prize, it obviously pleased some other people because of its treatment of race relations. Miss Smith wrote: "It is truly a big story—not only stretching back in time but big in the sense of its spiritual quality, its intellectual validity. Big, too, in the prophetic vision of a future that we cannot escape, big because the author has the moral toughness to probe into the dark corners of human experience." [19]

Among numerous other novels reviewed by Miss Smith were *Many Thousands Gone* by the Negro author, Ronald L. Fair, and *The Far Family* by Wilma Dykeman. As for Mr. Fair's book, Miss

Smith praised it, calling it "an enchanting deep South lie," and comparing it to *Purlie Victorious* by Ossie Davis. She also gave warm praise to Miss Dykeman's novel which delved into the history and development of a mountain family. But Miss Smith was not wholly satisfied with Howard Zinn's book, *The Southern Mystique*; and in her review she gave her reasons for dissatisfaction, saying that what was wrong was his "failures to see that racism is not merely a problem of prejudice, for it is a process of dehumanization that destroys not only love and dignity but one's respect for truth and one's willingness to live not as anarchic animals but as law-abiding human beings who are aware of what makes a man human and keeps him so."[20]

When Charles L. Weltner, a liberal congressman from Atlanta, Georgia, wrote his autobiography under the title *Southerner*, Miss Smith reviewed the book for the *Chicago Tribune*.[21] She discussed the political climate in Georgia and discussed again the characteristics of the mentally ill and the healthy-minded, the haters and non-haters. Although Mr. Weltner was liberal by political standards in Georgia, he was not liberal enough by Miss Smith's. She recognized, however, that, if he had been more liberal, he would never have been elected. She said he had won his seat in Congress the first time against "a man so caught in the feathers and molasses of sin-sex-and-segregation that he had no energy left to confront the urgently real needs of the large urban community he represented." She thought Mr. Weltner's book revealed his "rather shocking unawareness of the psychological ambiguities called 'the southern mind.' " She also concluded that he had not read widely enough in cultural and political history.

In addition to her feature articles in *Saturday Review*, Miss Smith frequently reviewed books for that magazine. In 1958, she reviewed *Stride Toward Freedom: The Montgomery Story* by Martin Luther King. She thought his book "the most interesting book that has come out of the current racial situation: important as documentary, full of accurate facts that historians will value; exciting as one dramatic scene after another unfolds: wise and compassionate in its point of view."[22]

Miss Smith reviewed *Tomorrow Is Now* by Eleanor Roosevelt, under the heading "Thoughts as Her Travels Ended."[23] This review, no doubt, was an effort of love and sadness for Lillian Smith. She had known Mrs. Roosevelt personally for many years, and it will be recalled that she had credited Mrs. Roosevelt's intercession with the president for getting the post office ban on *Strange Fruit* lifted over night. These two women, both courageous and determined fighters for Negro rights, had also exchanged numerous letters through the years. Miss Smith, who had carefully preserved her correspondence for some years, suffered a personal loss when her files were burned in 1955.

When she reviewed *American Women: The Changing Image*, edited by Beverly Benner Cassara, she found material in the book that supported her views regarding the status of American women: "We might as well face it: We women don't know who we are. Not only are we bereft of a public image we like; we don't have a private image of ourselves either."[24] In the Daniel interview, mentioned previously, she was reported as saying:

> I want, too, to do a volume of short stories about women. Women are so secretive. We have not told what we know about life. No truly great autobiography has been written by a woman—although Simone de Beauvoir has done awfully well at it.
>
> But we women must somehow learn to stop lying and tell ourselves and others the truth. Our mystery lies in part in our giant-size talent for lying.

Exactly what Miss Smith meant remains, however, a secret.

IV *The Self-Analyst*

Between 1949 and 1964, Lillian Smith published five nonfiction books. Three of them, *Killers of the Dream* (1949), *The Journey* (1954), and *Memory of a Large Christmas* (1962), recounted the personal experiences, feelings, and thoughts of the author; and they constitute Miss Smith's self-analysis. In the "Foreword: A Letter to My Publisher," which appeared in the Anchor Book edition of *Killers of the Dream* (1963), she explained that she had written the book for two reasons: first, to attempt to answer questions which had bothered her as a child and to try to reconcile the various aspects of her life; second, to explore the meaning of life in a segregated culture, to talk to herself about the effects of such a culture on her personally, and to try to understand the whole social context of life in the South.

Further explanation of what Miss Smith was doing in her writings may be derived from the following quotation from Ernst Cassirer, which appears on the title page of *The Journey*: "If I put out the light of my own personal experience I cannot see and I cannot judge the experience of others." Miss Smith believed in this approach to writing, and a study of her collected works indicates that she was personally and inextricably "in" everything that she wrote. Although *Strange Fruit* bears the earmarks of objectivity, the most obvious of which is the third-person point of view, its cargo is Lillian Smith and her messages, as a study of her total achievement readily shows. After *Strange Fruit*, with the exception of her short book *Our Faces, Our Words*, she abandoned the objective point of view altogether, writing from then on in the first person. She felt a need to turn the light upon herself, and in this she was extremely successful. One problem, which is not uncommon in self-analytical writing, is that Miss Smith repeated herself frequently, sometimes using identical words from one article or book to another.

After Miss Smith had studied herself thoroughly and repeatedly and had found what she believed to be the truth, she could not understand why others did not see and respond to what she saw. For instance, in the above-mentioned Foreword, she reviewed the triumph of communism in Cuba and elsewhere, speaking again of the harshness of colonialism, referring to Asian and African countries, and concluding that the United States would not be able to influence the attitudes of the people in those countries so long as it maintained white supremacy in public institutions. Then she asked: "Why don't we see this? Is there a tendency to blindness in those who overvalue their whiteness?" Then a few paragraphs later, she asked, "Why are we like this?" Although she used the rhetorical "we," Miss Smith had found the true way for herself; and she was impatient and frequently discouraged because others did not accept the truth of what she saw.

She was greatly disturbed by the apathy of Americans of the North, South, and West. Those who failed to act, she thought, were killing the American dream. They were not doing harm, but doing nothing could also kill. While she was discussing the death of the national dream which was inherent in the founding of the United States as a democratic society, she depicted most successfully the death of her personal dream, relating vividly the sense of loss and dissatisfaction in her childhood. She knew this very well, although she said in the Foreword, "I realize this is personal memoir, in one sense; in another sense, it is Every Southerner's memoir." Even so, her frustration throughout her writing career was caused in great part by the fact that she did not and could not speak for every Southerner. She said many times, and she truly believed, that every person's experience was his own, unique and incapable of being duplicated. *Killers of the Dream* is, therefore, valuable as Miss Smith's personal memoir, written when she was fifty-two years of age and while she was enjoying fame and fortune as a result of publishing *Strange Fruit*.

Killers of the Dream is divided into four parts, with the first sentence in each part containing the words *children or childhood*. It is apparent from this book, as well as from her notes and private conversations, that Lillian Smith never felt close to her mother. By the time her seventh child was born, Mrs. Smith would naturally have had many demands on her time. The most traumatic experience for the tiny Lillian, however, was the birth of her younger sister, Esther, at which time Lillian was turned over to the care of a Negro nurse. She remembered the nurse as being a loving and attentive person. But in addition to Lillian's feeling of rejection by her mother, she pictured Mrs. Smith as a person who did not understand her children and their needs. She remembered her mother as a vague, inarticulate person who may have been disillusioned with her life in Jasper but who never revealed her intimate feelings. Miss Smith's frustrating relationship with her mother was heightened after the death of Mr. Smith in 1930 when Lillian had major responsibility for her ailing mother until Mrs. Smith's death in 1938.

Miss Smith portrayed her father as a dedicated Methodist who once kept the whole family kneeling in prayer, continuing "his talk with God," while the fire whistle sounded louder and louder at his mill. He was so strongly opposed to the sale of liquor in Jasper that he openly lined up his employees, white and Negro, and gave each a silver dollar to vote for prohibition.

As for being one of nine children, Miss Smith recalled: "We had our times of anxiety of course, for there were hard lessons to be learned about the soul and 'bad things' to be learned about sex. Sometimes I have wondered how we learned them with a mother so shy with words." It might be conjectured, to take a Freudian line, that Lillian Smith spent her life overcompensating for the shyness of her mother by boldly using any word in the realms of sex or soul.

For one whose mother was mute in the face of personal matters, Miss Smith went to the other extreme, never hesitating to talk or write about whatever touched on human life. And one has to conclude that she believed in shock as a means of reforming the South.

At the time of its publication, one review pointed out that *"Killers of the Dream* is badly organized, excessively repetitious and too persistently eloquent; reading it is somewhat like eating seven courses of soufflé."* The book is, indeed, eloquent as only Lillian Smith could be when she was recalling her childhood experiences or analyzing human problems. She faltered when she undertook to give answers to other people's questions. As the above criticism indicates, however, *Killers of the Dream* is badly organized. In each major section, Miss Smith started over again with childhood and moved forward to the contemporary dilemma, searching along the way for new ramifications to the South's problems and frequently repeating herself. The organization of this and other books by Lillian Smith is representative of her elliptical thinking. By her eloquent manipulation of the language she returned again and again to the same subjects, leaving the reader somewhere under the bridge wondering why she took the return trip.

Miss Smith had a great deal to say about white mothers relegating their children to the care of Negro nurses. Taking a psychological approach to the matter, she reasoned that white males through the years have been inclined to sexual relationships with colored women because they are searching for their mothers and trying to return to the arms of their old Negro nurses. Another psychological interpretation, which is just as plausible as Miss Smith's, is that a young man like Tracy Deen in *Strange Fruit*, through some kind of guilt about sex, cannot make a sexual relationship with a woman whom he considers to be his social equal. As this theory goes, he must feel superior to his sexual mate. There are, no doubt, as many such explanations as there have been relationships, but Lillian Smith enjoyed generalizing on such subjects, and she spoke with authority regarding her point of view, which was her privilege, of course. At any rate, she made vivid her discussion by calling these relationships "ghost relationships": "Three ghost relationships—white man and colored woman, white father and colored children, white child and his beloved colored nurse—haunting the mind of the South and giving shape to our lives and our souls."

Miss Smith's resentment of the primness of her own mother sometimes caused her to make exaggerated claims for the child-rearing methods of Negro mothers. She thought that the wrong lessons on money, sex, sin, and segregation were taught by white parents. But the children of their Negro servants "were having recess from lessons, and for reasons no one could understand were healthy and serene in nature, less aggressive, less greedy than the white children." This evaluation of the happiness of Negro children might have been voiced by any segregationist who wanted to prove that Negroes were fun-loving, contented people who did not need education or the things white children had.

That was not what Miss Smith meant. She was making a point about the psychology of raising children. She went on to say that among the Negro children, life was "naked and unashamed." She wrote: "Little black children did all the naughty things little white children were punished for, did them and prospered in body and mind." Miss Smith was remarkably impressed with the success of Negro mothers in the rearing of their own children:

> I think these old black matriarchs knew secrets of child rearing and of sanity that our psychiatrists have been learning the hard way for the past sixty years through research, and that white mothers still know too little about. . . . these women knew intuitively, or from old lore, the psychosomatic truths that we whites are groping awkwardly toward today. The results in their children were a stability, a health, a capacity for accepting strain, an exuberance, and a lack of sadism and guilt that no Anglo-Saxon group, to my knowledge, has ever shown.

In another chapter, Miss Smith spoke again of the misery of Southern white women and of the fact that they turned their children over to the care of Negro nurses. She contended, however, that the white mothers did this unwillingly and that they were made unhappy in later life by their sons' (she makes no statement about daughters) loving the nurse more than they loved their mothers. She was firmly convinced that Southern white women of her mother's generation were hollow, long-suffering people who tried to comfort themselves with religion.

With the maturity of Lillian's own generation, however, Southern women were less helpless and began to take action on their own initiative. It was in 1930 that the Association of Southern Women for the Prevention of Lynching was formed with the willing support of some of the male members of the women's families. According to Miss Smith, this association had a measure of success because Dr. Will Alexander, as long ago as 1918, had led a group of men and women in forming the first interracial committee in the South. It will be recalled that Dr. Alexander's work led eventually to the founding of the Southern Regional Council, which has continued to function effectively throughout the South.

In this chapter, Miss Smith oscillated between the history of the Ku Klux Klan, Negro leadership, and the efforts of white women to eradicate lynching, and then returned to the psychological situation of women: "We cannot forget that their culture had stripped these white mothers of profound biological rights, had ripped off their inherent dignity and made them silly statues and psychic children, stunting their capacity for understanding and enjoyment of husbands and family."

Toward the end of the chapter, she took a new tack, indicating confusion on her part as to just what it was she wished to say about the ineffectuality of women and just who it was that should be blamed. Maybe, she thought, mothers had been blamed too much for the failures of their children. She concluded that somebody, centuries ago, must have decided that women were inferior to men and that they should therefore be deprived of equal sexual, political, and economic rights. She called Saint Paul a misogynist and expressed the thought that women's trials may have begun in protest against the "ancient matriarch."

In one chapter, "Distance and Darkness," Miss Smith reviewed the history of the rural South, the isolation of rural people, and generally discussed situations and facts that may have become familiar to the reader through history books and W. J. Cash's *Mind of the South*. This material is not redundant in *Killers of the Dream*, but its familiarity from other sources for the educated reader gives the sensation of repetition.

Much of the material in the first chapter had been published in *Common Ground* in 1943, and the whole of the chapter entitled "Two Men and a Bargain" had been published in *South Today* in 1943. This last item is intended to dramatize a silent conspiracy between Mr. Rich White and Mr. Poor White to relegate the Negro to second-class citizenship. Her point is that the wealthy white Southerner, for economic reasons, has used the poor white man to keep the Negro in subjugation. The wealthy white man accomplished this by convincing the poor and ignorant white man that he was better than the Negro and that it was better for everybody if the wealthy man kept control of the sources of money, and gave a modicum of elevation and superiority to the poor white man who carried out the lynchings and other intimidations required by the social structure. The parable and Miss Smith's message are wasted on the reader because she did not fully understand the economic pressures of which she spoke. She had, for the most part, avoided economics in her writings; she chose to explain the world's problems on psychological and sociological levels.

In the final section of the book, she reviewed again the contemporary situation in the South, mentioning the symbols of segregation, the white primary, the Confederate flag, the failings of the preachers, editorial writers, and politicians, saying again that there were always a few who did not follow the herd on segregation. Then she upbraided the Fugitive-Agrarian writers, as she had done in other contexts, charging that no writers in literary history had failed their region as completely as they had. She found their works, including lectures, talk, and writings, so inaccurate that it was difficult for her to ferret out the facts about them.

She did, with effort, construct a substantial list of their characteristics, which may be summarized as follows: (1) They recognized that industrialization would damage society; but they failed to see that it was not necessary, with the coming of industry to the South, to worship material things or science. (2) Their minds were not so cultured as the tone in which they spoke, and it was too bad that they were having great influence on young people. (3) They "urged their students to busy themselves with literary dialectics, to support the 'New Criticism' instead of a new life; and one way to do this was to search the pages of contemporary turgid writing for secret symbolic meanings where no meaning existed." (4) Their tone, which was Southern, echoed post-World War I German thinking. (5) They failed to understand that slavery had already brought about the dehumanization they feared from science. (6) They might have provided brilliant leadership for the South, but they chose to deal with trivial matters. (7) They contended that "the role of artist does not embrace concern and action. They are wrong."

In her final chapter, "The Chasm and the Bridge," Miss Smith took up another favorite subject which she saw as having two worrisome aspects. She was disturbed by the chasm between individuals and groups, but she was also concerned with man's internal chasm—the split which she saw in the individual personality. There is a chasm, too, between past and future; and there are others, real and imaginary, which she would like to have seen bridged. The spirit of man, she thought, has been ignored in the modern scientific age when almost everybody demands proof before accepting any experience as true. There are some experiences involving the soul, she believed, which cannot be proved and modern man is wrong to ignore them.

She concluded that science had found numerous ways to compress time and to get things done on earth, but too little attention was being given to art and philosophy and the further development of man himself. She wrote: "It is possible that the Devil is luring us into outer space to divert us from this project of evolving a new being. But perhaps we are capable of both giant tasks. To try either of them without tapping our moral and psychic resources, and without safeguarding the soul in us would be an irreversible mistake."

She also discussed the need for symbols in life, but she cited the damage that the "mythic mind" can do to itself and the world if it goes wild over symbols. At this point, Miss Smith was following the ideas of Karl Jung and applying them to the white-supremacy theory, saying that man's mythic mind was responsible for this false theory. She was convinced that the average man could lose himself in the ramifications of his mythic mind and perhaps never escape. Only the artist could disentangle himself and others because he knew how to use his mythic mind to create healthy, useful symbols. Furthermore, Miss Smith thought it was the duty of the artist to undertake the leadership of man; and, since she considered herself an artist, it was obvious that she was doing her best to help white supremacists see the light.

Although Lillian Smith, at one time or another, saw all kinds of dehumanizing forces at work, including science, industrialization, war, communism, and demagoguery, she gave most attention to the dehumanizing effects of white supremacy. White supremacy cuts both ways. In one, the white man has dehumanized the Negro by treating him as if he were an animal; incapable of citizenship; and unworthy of respect, position, and reward for his labor. In a second, the white man, through his treatment of the Negro and through his devotion to the idea that white skin is superior to dark skin, has dehumanized himself. This dehumanization begins to work on white children at a very young age, according to Miss Smith.

Miss Smith had her own notion of the sanctity of the human being which she had gleaned from ancient ideas that have come down to modern man through religion, poetry, and politics. She believed that if the idea of the sanctity of man should turn out to be merely a bedtime story then earth and its population would come to an end. She concluded *Killers of the Dream* by raising the question as to whether mankind has the desire to reach for a dream, presumably a dream of true humanization. She thought of her book as one small fragment in the history of a period when man might begin to separate himself from nature and take charge of his own evolution.

In *The Journey* Lillian Smith wrote again about herself, her experiences, her thoughts, her hopes. The journey was both literal and symbolic: the real one took her on a visit to parts of Georgia which she had known in her youth; The other one she described as follows: "What I sought, of course, was something to believe in; something that intelligence and heart can accept, something that can fuse past and future, and art and science, and God and one's self into a purposeful whole."

She was puzzled by man's endurance, his hope in the face of what she called his "brokenness." She also marveled at his creative spirit. Through the years, in addition to her concern over the handicaps which racial coloring and mental illness inflict upon human beings, she became more and more preoccupied with physical handicaps and with man's ability to overcome them. In her search of "the faith to believe that we can fulfill our role in this evolving universe of which we have been given such awesome glimpses," Miss Smith made systematic observations of human beings under the stress of survival, especially those in rehabilitation centers who were making the supreme effort to overcome physical disabilities. She also studied great works of art and read poetry and philosophy.

In *The Journey*, she was, of course, talking about herself and the things that puzzled and interested her; and talking about herself was the thing that Lillian Smith did very well. As in *Killers of the Dream*, she made seemingly insignificant people and experiences live; and she wrote eloquently of them because they were extremely important to her. As in her previous books, she moved forward and backward, without concern for chronology or without any obvious organizational pattern. There is no index for this or any of Miss Smith's books. She was a demanding writer; she demanded that the reader go with her and have all the experiences she had. It is a measure of her talent that she succeeded in taking the reader with her, even on the most trivial excursions.

In the first chapter of *The Journey*, she discussed her childhood experiences with crippled and retarded children to show how persons who are different are rejected by society. Walls similar to those erected between the races have been erected against groups with physical and mental defects. Likewise, she thought, the scholarly, the creative, or the meditative person may be walled off from society because of his differences. In addition to wanting society to accept all members of the human race and become whole, Miss Smith wondered why man, individual man, could not be whole. She thought he could heal the split in himself and become a whole being by constantly demanding of himself the utmost of creative will in the evolutionary struggle.

Miss Smith, a great admirer of Martha Graham, took unusual pleasure in the perfection of physical motion which Miss Graham's dancing represented. Through dancing man can, according to Miss Smith, perfect his control over his physical body, and it is perfection in any form which gave pleasure to Lillian Smith. Imperfections in man's behavior, mind, body, or society were burdensome to her; and she went on a lifelong journey to satisfy herself that man was on his way to perfection. Belief in the perfectibility of mankind may have lost favor in this century with most people, but Miss Smith needed such a belief; and she struggled to maintain hers.

In the third chapter, Miss Smith told of an actual trip through the coastal areas of Georgia where her parents had been reared. In the process of visiting and describing the country, she laced the chapter with memories, discussing the life of the Negro in the Deep South, his churches, his songs, his laughter, his segregation from white society. She took to task the "power-hungry censors who try to dehumanize man"—those who were banning from television, radio, and stage what is "misnamed 'racial and religious stereotypes,'" a phrase which she thought was being used at that time to cover anything that did not flatter a group's image of itself. Despite the sincerity of some of the people in charge of publishing and broadcasting outlets, Miss Smith thought that they were distorting reality by insisting that no Negro should be depicted as doing domestic service. She said that it all amounted to a new racial "line" which permitted the portrayal of a white girl in love with a Negro man, but not the opposite; and thus a new stereotype was being created.

Lillian Smith always believed in depicting reality, regardless of its flaws; and, in her opinion, to censor out certain types of characters was to disfigure the work of art.

In the fourth chapter, she described a small graveyard where she had stopped on her journey through Georgia. Eight children's graves with no adult graves in the yard caused Miss Smith to meditate upon the possible fate of the parents. She also recalled the past when medicine offered few cures and when death came frequently to every family—the times before X-ray, vaccines, blood plasma, and antibiotics. She gave a moving account of the isolation and suffering of rural Americans before the advent of preventive medicine and miracle drugs. She recalled how, before World War I, fevers plagued the country in hot weather and pneumonia and other lung diseases killed quickly in cold weather. Because people did not know how to cure themselves, she said, "there was as much foolish talk and absurd precautions taken as are taken today against that unknown enemy 'communism.'" When death came in those sad times, there was always, it seemed, the odor of gardenias, an odor strongly familiar to all native Southerners. There must have been funerals when gardenias were not in bloom, but the association of that odor with funerals has persisted.

Miss Smith devoted one chapter to a review of her youthful obsession with science, her insistence upon facts, and her refusal to believe in miracles of the biblical type. She came, she said, finally to realize that the process of "understanding" can be miraculous: "Now, one by one, we are returning from that flight from the unknown. Humbled, some of us; not rejecting science but no longer demanding certainty as if it were a human right; beginning once more to put the puzzle together, hoping this time that we shall not leave out the human being and his relationships with himself and with God as we almost did before."

She concluded that man had to have faith in order to sustain himself in difficult situations, but he also had to have doubt in order to continue his search for truth. Faith and doubt must work together, she thought, in order for man to get "around the unknown curve." If too much reliance on faith could result in disappointment, doubt could be a force for evil when the doubter merely undermines the faithful and spreads suspicion of the future. But doubt, when it leads to new knowledge, is a force for good. She was, therefore, convinced that mankind must have the capacity for belief, the willingness to accept some things on faith, if he is to have the courage and hope to move into the future; but he must also have doubt if he is to ask the questions which will result in new answers and increased knowledge:

So it goes. I wonder why it is so hard for us to accept these two partners out of which comes life, this dualism out of which unity is created. There is always a question, and an answer, before knowledge is found. We know everything creative that concerns human existence comes in pairs: freedom and responsibility, faith and doubt, the question and the answer, risk and security, the child and his grown-up self, past and future, wonder and certainty, pain and pleasure, male and female, sex and love, the dream and reality, victory and defeat, man and God. Keep them together, we have a whole, we have life; cut them apart, we find death at the center. Maybe this is the meaning of sin: for human beings to cut these deep relationships in two.

A large portion of the center of the book is devoted to reminiscences of the Smith grandmother and of her relationships with her nine sons, of whom Lillian's father was a favorite. Being interested in the ways in which anxiety is created in children, Miss Smith told about three little children, two boys and a girl, discovering their sexual differences and the shame which the mother created by scolding them. She also revealed a special talent for describing motel operators, in their different species, whom she had met on her tour of several days through the countryside.

In her concern for the wholeness of man, physically, mentally, and spiritually, Miss Smith expressed high regard for physicians, particularly surgeons, who work to restore the physical body. In *The Journey*, she recounted a conversation she had had with a friend whose young son had lost both arms in an accident. The mother had the usual symptoms of guilt about her son's disability, and she suffered a common revulsion at the sight of his handicap. Although the child made a good adjustment, the mother required some months of adjustment before she could handle her full role in his life again.

In commenting upon the friend having left her son temporarily because she could not face her responsibility, Miss Smith said: "But it seemed to me that, this time, it was not so much a flight as a search. Something in her words, primitive, irrational, but human and natural, had rushed out after those arms just as a mother would leave her other children to find the child who is lost. The rest of Bill was *there*. It could wait. What was lost had to be recovered. So that he could be whole again. So that she could be whole again." When the same friend's husband was killed in war, Miss Smith drew some conclusions about life and death. She had greatly admired the husband because of his attitude toward life, his ability to accept tragedy along with joy; and she wrote, "I believe every good life has a good relationship with death."

In trying to analyze the meaning of *honor*, she decided that not everybody had the wisdom or the courage to be "a quality person," but there were, nevertheless, a large number of people who did have the requisites. For those who did not have what it takes to be a "quality person," there was art; and these persons could look and listen and be related to greatness. She believed in art for man's sake and not for the sake of religion, or beauty, or even art itself. She contended that art is an experience, both for the creator and for the observer, one of man's most profound experiences.

Miss Smith's conclusions on the meaning of life, as she stated them at the end of *The Journey*, do not satisfy many people. The devoutly religious reader will not accept them, and the skeptical intellectual will say that she concluded her journey at the point where he would have begun. Still, it was her journey; and she was satisfied with her own facing of life, saying finally "this is what man's journey is about, I think." The heart of her conclusion lies in her contention that man must face reality and know when dream is dream, that he must be willing to go the extra mile in troubled times, that each trial must be accepted as preparation for the next one, and that he must have faith even though he cannot have answers to unanswerable questions.

With her little book, *Memory of a Large Christmas*, Lillian Smith rounded out her memoirs of childhood in the South. This reminiscence, first published in *Life* magazine, is a mellow and sentimental recalling of the excitement and associations which glorified the Christmas season for her, a little girl in a large family. Her excitement and pleasure in the activities of her brothers and sisters are easily transmitted to the reader, who cannot help but wish that she had called them by their names rather than labeling them Age Thirteen, Age Fifteen, and so on.

Hog-killing in the family backyard fascinated Miss Smith through the years, and her description of when and how to go about the job is detailed enough to assure the success of any amateur hog-killer. She had a natural talent, too, for describing the atmosphere, foods, decorations, and odors of the Christmas season in a part of the country where there is often frost but where Christmas Day may be warm and sunny. If Christmas in Jasper, when the family was important and affluent, thrilled with its mystery and surprises, Christmas after the family had lost its money and moved to the summer cottage at Clayton became a challenge.

Miss Smith recorded fond memories of how her father made the best of the sad experience of losing his businesses. The same sort of thing happened to numerous exporters of lumber and naval stores when the European markets were cut off with the approach of World War I. As Miss Smith pointed out, her family was not alone in being poor in a region where poverty was widely known and understood. But Mr. Smith had a deep religious faith and an ebullience in life which helped him through the most dismal experiences.

During one of their austere Christmas seasons in Clayton, the head of the house decided to invite the chain gang to have dinner with the family. Forty-eight criminals, wearing stripes and under guard, marched down to the Smith backyard where Mr. Smith read the Bible to them and wished them and their families a happy Christmas. Then the women of the family served plates which a murderer, a rapist, and a bank-robber passed among the other men.

The last section of *Memory of a Large Christmas* is a description of a "Christmas Kitchen Fifty Years Ago." After utilizing her eye for detail to give a vivid descripton of the space, equipment, and personnel of the kind of kitchen she knew as a child, Miss Smith gave a few favorite recipes. Some of them, such as the ones for ambrosia and coconut cake, are still commonly used in Southern kitchens at Christmastime.

V *The Social Analyst*

In addition to the three biographical works already discussed, Miss Smith published two other nonfiction books, *Now Is the Time* (1955) and *Our Faces, Our Words* (1964). Both of these books are concerned with racial integration in the United States, and *Now Is the Time* was written immediately following the 1954 Supreme Court decision on school integration. As she had indicated in her previous writings, Lillian Smith was gravely concerned for the welfare of America's children, both white and Negro; and she had felt for many years that segregation was just as damaging to one as to the other. She was warm in her praise of Chief Justice Warren who delivered the court's unanimous opinion that the public schools in the United States should be integrated: "He stated, for the first time in the history of a country's highest court, that a child's feelings are important to a nation; that shame and rejection can block a mind from learning, hence segregation is a barrier to human growth which no state in our democracy can maintain legally in its public school system."

She reviewed some of the causes of the fear that American citizens, both in the North and in the South, have of integration. She said that the word "segregation" had numerous synonyms: "isolation, censorship, restriction, withdrawal, Jim Crow, caste, imprisonment, quarantine, repression," and that they are all used by man to cut himself off from some part of the world for his own security, even though the danger might be only imaginary. She pointed out again, as she had on other occasions, that the mentally and physically handicapped were also segregated from society, frequently by state law.

With regard to segregation and the Negro, Miss Smith expressed her view that the white man's anxiety derived from the conflict between "his Christian beliefs and slavery." Then came the Civil War, which helped the Negro a little but which caused such misery in the South that demagoguery thrived, thus leading to the modern pedicament. She deplored the lack of responsible leadership in the South between 1865 and 1920, citing only two voices for which she had respect: those of General Robert E. Lee and George Washington Cable.

The Supreme Court decision which declared unconstitutional the segregation of public schools was handed down in May, 1954. All thinking people, including Lillian Smith, felt that the long summer months would give people time to think over and get used to the idea that Negro and white children would and should attend the same schools in the fall. In the border states and in Washington, D.C., the school boards decided to integrate. In the words of Miss Smith: "In the good American way, they went ahead on this new frontier, exploring, taking risks; with courage and independence they began to work things out."

She also pointed out that "freedom can be freedom to do wrong as easily as it can be freedom to do right—unless our country's laws are obeyed." When students, at the prompting of their parents, went on strike at various schools, Miss Smith pointed out that there were not many thousands of these students and parents, but that there were "enough for us to see what it looks like when American citizens put their allegiance to their color above the Constitution of the United States." Like people all across the country, she was shocked by the behavior of white people who seemed bent upon depriving Negro children of their rights: "We began to realize that a nation is no better than the people in it; its strength is no greater than the beliefs in their hearts and the values they hold to." This situation was hard for her to believe, even though it had been said so often that the words rang like a rusty, clanging cliché.

School intregration was a challenge to the American people to do some soul-searching, to strengthen themselves and their beliefs, to demonstrate democracy at work, and to win friends throughout the world by rectifying an old and terrible mistake, according to Miss Smith. She warmly and comfortingly acknowledged that everybody—individuals, groups, nations—can make mistakes; but only honorable people can meet the tests of correcting errors. She cited the wisdom of the Founding Fathers who had "created a Constitution that was and still is a living, growing thing: resilient, flexible, sensitive to the fact that men change as they gain knowledge of their world and of themselves."

Obviously, Miss Smith hoped that the Supreme Court decision on segregation would result in widespread acknowledgment of the error of segregation, particularly in the South; but, if she foresaw the long struggle that was ahead, if she suspected that at least four new civil rights laws would be required in the ensuing twelve years to effect any substantial changes in the plight of the American Negro, she did not say so. She was sounding a hopeful note which she thought might be contagious—that might reach people that she had been unable to reach before.

She reviewed the historical facts of the enactment of segregation laws in the South between 1881 and 1907, even while the Negroes spoke out for their rights, "eloquently, in prayer, song, poetry, art, books." It was another type of speaking out, however, which had resulted in the May 17, 1954, decision of the court; it was what Miss Smith called "the brilliant work of the Legal Committee of the National Association for the Advancement of Colored People." She thought that this organization, despite the fact that it had been

111

sneered at, charged with being Communist, and otherwise abused, had made history in securing rights for black people by using democratic means.

Segregation had been a wall between people; it was only one of the walls against which Lillian Smith had been fighting since her return from China in 1925, but she saw it as an artificial barrier supported by no psychological or sociological rationale. The white man had not been able, she thought, to reconcile his belief in freedom with his treatment of the Negro; but this failure in reconciliation led, over a long period of time, to attempts at assuaging guilt by defending white supremacy, an idea which could not be defended. It was a long, sad period in the history of the Western white man, of democracies, and of colonialism, as Miss Smith said repeatedly.

In the South, despite the long, hard period of Reconstruction, Miss Smith thought that political leaders and plain citizens had indulged too long and too willingly in self-pity. By pitying themselves and blaming others, the South and its leaders had neglected to take the steps required to move into the modern world. Demagogues, with the assent of the people, passed poll-tax laws, instituted literacy tests, and talked of "mongrelizing" the races, until the point of no return had been reached in the South. Miss Smith compared racial segregation to cancer as a destructive force in the healthy body of democracy.

The legal barriers were serious enough, but she said, "We cannot, even yet, assess the harm done by the walls that were put up in minds, North and South." Her point was that the insistence upon racial segregation caused white people to refuse to listen to new ideas, to pass laws against the teaching of evolution in the schools, and to deny scientific truth at all levels. Intellectual honesty in young people was derided, and intellectual honesty in ministers and teachers was punished by threats of dismissal or actual dismissal from their positions. Miss Smith had witnessed in her own lifetime the various means by which white citizens closed off the avenues to new knowledge and insight and continued to defend the immoral practice of segregation.

Lillian Smith was convinced that, during the first quarter of this century, numerous white Southerners had changed their views about segregation. She herself, having been reared in a family where segregation had been taught quietly and in a "well-bred" way, was evidence of her belief that change was occurring, but in silence and loneliness for the most part. Thousands of Southerners, like Miss Smith's oldest sister, members of orthodox religious groups, went to China, India, Africa, Japan, and South America as missionaries. With distance and with their experiences of racial differences giving them material for thought, these people could not help but change their thinking about their region's treatment of the Negro; but these were gentle people who thought their thoughts and obeyed the laws of segregation. Miss Smith wrote: "And we remained silent. Silence was our gift to the demagogue. Year after year, we gave him this large present. We laughed at demagoguery; we were secretly outraged by it; we knew the demagogue was a disgrace and a danger to our region and our nation and our world—but each year we underwrote his activities with our silence."

Although missionaries who had returned from their journeys and those thinking people who had stayed home kept their peace, rarely putting into words thoughts which would have been subversive by some legal and political standards, Miss Smith sensed a current: "The current of history was flowing swiftly now toward wholeness. And we finally, somehow, got in it. The walls were crumbling fast; distance, ignorance, language—all these were giving way." Miss Smith's reference to "wholeness" was in the nature of her thinking about the human being as a civilized one. She saw man as making the most of his humanity and his capacity for growth only when he lived in a society which was not fragmented by racial barriers, when he was individually mentally and physically whole and up to the task of being human, and when he could move freely among the peoples of the world without arrogance or fear. This idealistic vision for man, though it is not unique with her and though some people see it woven into the United Nations Charter, was at the heart of Lillian Smith's writing and thinking between 1936 and 1966. It was no little dream for her region or for Negroes only or for white people only; it was a vision she had for a potential society of men on earth.

The New Deal was a force for significant change in the South, despite the uproar from those who wanted the region, for selfish purposes, to remain unchanged. Miss Smith regarded the federal government's health, school, farm, and employment programs as having given encouragement to thousands of economically deprived black and white people. When Negroes and whites met with

Mrs. Roosevelt in 1938 to discuss mutual problems, cries of "communism" rose from all corners of the region. Miss Smith always thought it strange that Americans had so frequently failed to give Christianity or democracy, or both, the credit for constructive programs in this country. Programs which tended to serve minority groups or the helpless poor were believed by those who do not need them to be Communist inspired; and this attitude was a strange kind of credit for haters of communism to be rendering to the enemy, as Miss Smith observed.

In citing the gradual changes which had taken place in the South during the 1930's and 1940's, Miss Smith failed to document some of the historical happenings which arouse interest in the reader not already familiar with them—and this fault pervades all of Miss Smith's nonfiction writing. In her hurried summarizing of events, she neglected to give names, places, and titles which future readers would need in order to be properly oriented. The following is an example of her technique in *Now Is the Time*: "Two novels were written—one by a Negro Southerner, one by a white Southerner—which shocked the country into giving grave thought to its human relationships." Which novels did Miss Smith have in mind? Probably modesty prevented her from mentioning *Strange Fruit*, but the reader would have to hazard a guess that she was referring to her own work. And what was the other novel? Could it have been *Native Son* by Richard Wright? Surely modesty did not keep her from mentioning Wright and other writers of the period, but the reader now can only guess that she had Wright in mind.

She also wrote that "In 1942 the first editorial in the South against race segregation appeared in a small magazine." Unless one is familiar with *South Today* and with Lillian E. Smith's own editorial, entitled "Are We Not All Confused?," discussed in Chapter 2 of this study, he can only wonder where the editorial appeared and who wrote it. He may also wonder, if he has not done extensive research on the matter, whether Miss Smith's statement is accurate. As with most little magazines, files of *South Today* twenty years after publication ceased are scarce. Even the editors did not own complete files of the magazine, a fact which, coupled with Miss Smith's vague references to her sources of information, makes verification unnecessarily tedious for scholars.

In the fifteen years prior to the 1954 Supreme Court decision about integration in the public schools, startling changes in race relations had been taking place in the United States. Miss Smith cited the following: (1) removal of the poll tax in several Southern states; (2) the white primary was ruled unconstitutional by the Supreme Court; (3) other court rulings permitted Negroes to use sleeping and dining cars on railroads in the South; (4) court decisions on various test cases had influence on hiring practices and had decreased discrimination in employment; (5) Negroes had been admitted to several state colleges and universities in the South; (6) certain restrictive covenants on property had been declared unconstitutional by the Supreme Court; (7) church schools, notably the Catholic ones, were beginning to accept Negro students; (8) professional societies and fraternities were beginning to lift their barriers to integration; (9) some national organizations integrated their memberships; (10) some Northern states enacted civil rights laws to break down extralegal segregation; (11) radio and television programs were being integrated; (12) Actors Equity and professional baseball were doing their part to open the theater and sports to all races; (13) restaurants and hotels in Washington, D.C., were desegregated in 1953; and (14) by 1954 the armed forces of the United States had desegrated all aspects of life on military bases, even in the South.

Hers was a hopeful summary of changes as she looked forward to implementation of the Supreme Court's decision on the public schools. She thought that "*Now is the time* . . . to take out of the demagogues' hands forever a weapon too dangerous for this atomic age." Her contention was that *color* and *communism* were working together to destroy freedom throughout the world. And in the seventh chapter of *Now Is the Time*, Miss Smith again turned to one of her favorite subjects: the success of communism in the Far East. She thought the reason communism appealed to Asians and democracy did not could be explained in two words: "poverty" and "color." Her experience in China and India had made her realize that, while Americans, particularly those resident in the South, had experienced severe poverty at various times, only a small percentage of the total population had ever suffered the extreme deprivation of the sort that Asians constantly endured.

Again, as she had said in her comments in *South Today*, the colonial powers were not wholly responsible for poverty in Asia; but their exploitation of the resources and the people had added to the human burdens in that area. Asians were living in ignorance and disease when the colonial powers came upon the scene, so that colonialism could not be held responsible for causing these sufferings. But for two centuries, according to Miss Smith, the colonial powers had failed to make use of educational and medical techniques to relieve suffering in Asia. She also charged that, when industrialism came to the Western world, the colonial powers "deliberately restrained" industrial development in Asia in order to "hold these markets for their own manufactured goods."

To Miss Smith, the white man had not only failed to help Asians relieve their suffering, but he had humiliated them in other ways: "For the white colonial was often an arrogant man. Even at his best, he was quietly patronizing, subtly superior—using his white color like a flag in crises small and large, hoisting it above these proud peoples, blandly disregarding their ancient cultures, or, more likely, unaware of the vast and magnificent contributions they had made in the past to world civilization." She thought that, for the most part, these white colonials were gentlemanly, considerate men in their own countries and that, abroad, they simply forgot that human beings, even though hungry, dirty, and ill-housed, still had feelings. For the most part, the good that was done by the colonial powers in Asia had been overshadowed by the hurt and the long-harbored resentment of the people there.

In the United States, Miss Smith said, antagonism had grown out of the Civil War and Reconstruction and out of segregation of the races in the South; but colonialism had committed a long list of sins in Asia and Africa over a two-hundred-year period. She thought that the Communists were exploiting the memories which Asians and Africans had of (1) the 1919 incident at Amritsar when the British killed hundreds and wounded thousands of Indians who were demonstrating for the freedom of their country; (2) the 1939 pledge not to speak out for India's independence which American missionaries were forced to take; (3) the "white only" signs over doors and parks in Asia and Africa; (4) the reservation of clubs and swimming pools for Europeans only; (5) the issuance of passes for natives in South Africa to travel in their own country; (6) the imprisonment of native leaders such as Nehru, Madame Pandit, and Gandhi; (7) the white man's backyard, puritanistic treatment of Eurasians and Anglo-Indians; and (8) the "divide-and-weaken policies" of colonizing powers.

Communism had been successful in Asia, according to Lillian

Smith, by smoothly and seductively allowing the people to feel important. The Communists had mastered the demagogic techniques: "A good demagogue does not clamp a chain on the people; he persuades them to put it on themselves. He does not set up a secret police to hound you (not at first); he reminds you that to show your loyalty to him you must suspect your neighbor, even your family; you must set yourself up as a secret police. He does not put you on trial; he persuades you to put others on trial; he lets you pass judgment on the loyalty of everybody but yourself, and lets others pass judgment on you."

Citing the fact that the United States had had a minimal role in the colonization of foreign countries, Miss Smith posed a question as to why Americans were distrusted abroad. America was once a colony, which should have given Americans some understanding of the attitudes of colonized countries. To Miss Smith, the answer to her pondering was that "The United States' role in colonialism has been somewhat analogous to the North's role in American segregation: a matter, largely, of too many gentlemen's agreements and too much silent acquiescence. This is well known to Asians and Africans. We have supported colonial powers and their puppets when we should have been supporting democratic leaders of the people. This official vacillation of ours has again and again caused the Asian and African people's faith in our democratic integrity to be shaken."

Miss Smith expressed her conviction that Asian people did not like "white democracy" as it existed in the United States. Furthermore, they feared power as it was represented by the United States and by the hydrogen bomb. They well remembered that the first atomic bomb had been used against Asian people. According to Miss Smith, Asians did not fear Russia's hydrogen bomb because they did not believe Russia would ever use it against Asians. The predicament of the United States with regard to gaining the friendship of the Chinese, Indians, and other Asians was something akin to finding oneself in "a very small room with no exit." Miss Smith was hopeful, however, contending that there were numerous exits which could be opened if Americans were willing. She believed that any problem in the world could be solved, but the first step she advocated was the mystical one of belief: "If we could only believe" that "we" could solve the modern world's problems, then "we" could do it. She contended that all the difficulties "lie in our state of mind." If Americans would change their "state of mind" and abandon racial segregation immediately "the world's knotted state of mind will ease. Other strands will begin to loosen. Suspicion of the United States will diminish. Trust in American integrity will increase. Faith in our moral strength will return to us, too."

If this solution seemed too simple, she said, it should be considered as only the beginning. But it was the first step to which feeling people would respond readily and hopefully.

Then Miss Smith discussed her belief that all of earth's peoples were moving, inevitably, toward one great peaceful future. This century was an age in which walls had to be removed, in which man had to be concerned for his fellow man, in which free men had to work to prevent the spread of Communist tyranny, in which "chasms of ignorance and fear and distance and poverty" had to be replaced with their opposites. The choice for or against the One World idea, she thought, lay in the decisions which plain citizens made in the Western world.

In Part II of *Now Is the Time*, Miss Smith returned to the immediate problem of desegregation in the United States. She said that integration of the races would result in few noticeable changes in the external life of Americans; the biggest change would take place in the white man's way of thinking about race. In the meantime, to facilitate school integration and the general improvement of race relations, she asserted that there were things that even the most timid citizen could do. She cited a few "simple, undramatic things" which anybody could do: (1) treat Negroes with courtesy, using courtesy titles, and insist that local newspapers do the same; (2) refer to individual Negroes, not to "the Negro," and get to know individual Negroes, repeat praiseworthy information about them, visit their colleges, introduce white children to Negro adults and children; (3) write letters to the press, stores, hospitals, boards of education, and ministers suggesting ways in which race relations could be improved; (4) read books about Negroes and urge libraries, bookstores, clubs, and newspapers to publicize such books; (5) try to arrange for integrated groups to appear on local radio and television programs; (6) not be angered by race baiters; and (7) remember the things one should not say: "nigger," "darkie," or "coon"; discrediting race jokes; "don't repeat rumors of violence" or the old clichés about body odor, about the length of time required to remove segregation, about "the rights" of whites or blacks; and not try to speak for the South, but only for the individual self.

Miss Smith, of course, had high hopes for the immediate integration of all public schools; and it was her intention in her short book, *Now Is the Time*, to ease the fears of her compatriots and to smooth the way for whites and Negroes in the days and years ahead. She considered the fears of integration to be unfounded; they were products of "the land of ghosts" and would vanish when light was shone upon them. Obviously, she was trying to shine a bright light in order to rout anxiety and falsehood. She yearned for a situation in which white Americans would be willing to suffer the pangs of change in order to live creatively in a more healthy, productive society.

In Part III, she posed and answered twenty-five questions which had been asked of her, ones which were familiar to almost everybody, and which had been used in various distortions by demagogues to influence their audiences. This method was, of course, that of the teacher. Miss Smith was trying to reach and influence prejudiced white people because she thought that a large number of people would have to change their minds on several matters concerning the Negro citizen and racial integration. She grouped her questions and answers under eleven headings.

1. *Culture*. In answer to questions regarding separate cultures, the time required to civilize people, and the incidence of violence among Negroes, she said that all cultures were parts of the large human culture, thus each culture was dependent upon other cultures and upon the whole of human development. Most American Negroes, she pointed out, were born in America; and they developed in this civilized society in the same way and as readily as white people did. Regarding the incidence of violence among Negroes, she cited poverty, social rejection, poor schools, and unequal law enforcement as causes.

2. *Intermarriage and "Blood" and Inheritance*. In answer to a question on mongrelization of the races, Miss Smith said "There is only one race: the human race." Even though she discussed various aspects of what it meant to be human, her answer was the kind that fed the charge that Miss Smith believed in intermarriage. It was not enough for her to say that one race was not superior to another; she seemed to delight in squelching whatever pride any race might have in itself.

In answer to the commonly raised question, "Would you want your sister to marry a Negro?," Miss Smith wrote: "If a girl asked my advice I would say this: the quality of the man you marry, his values, tastes, habits, health, ability to make a living, sense of humor, intelligence, his anxieties, his interests, are far more important to you than the color of his skin or the name of his religion. It is, above all else, important that you love him. If you are mature and have chosen a mature man, you can weather the storms that will come from crossing the barriers." This answer was not one which pleased very many Negro or white people.

When she was asked if she thought "mixed marriages fair to children," she gave the logical answer that children born to married parents would be considerably better off than the millions of children who have been born out of wedlock and rejected by their fathers and their communities. Miss Smith, with her interest in the well-being of all children, had long sympathized with the plight of children of white men and Negro women in the South.

3. *Change and the Law*. In response to those people who said that education was better than legislation for solving race relations, Miss Smith wisely pointed out that both were necessary. The questions which she had heard and answered many times were usually loaded, as the following indicates: "What right has the government to invade our homes and tell us we must socialize with each other?" She answered: "Every American citizen has two kinds of rights: public and private. It is more often the citizen than the government that becomes confused about these rights. When the Supreme Court ruled legal segregation unconstitutional it was protecting the *public rights* of a minority against a majority, in certain states, that had taken those rights away." In response to complaints that the law should be consistent and the Supreme Court was merely playing politics when it reversed the *Plessy* decision of 1896, Miss Smith said, "The law is not an embalmed corpse: it is a living thing, changing as human conditions change, growing as man's conscience grows."

4. *God and the Bible*. The question as to why God did not make all men the same color if he wanted them to mix had been asked frequently by ignorant and prejudiced churchgoers. Miss Smith answered it with a question: "If God had not wanted people of different colors to mate, why didn't He make it biologically impossible for them to do so?" Furthermore, she said, the Bible is clear in calling for brotherhood and love and concern among men, with no place in its concepts for segregation.

120

5. *Economics*. Those who believed that the racial problem was largely economic, Miss Smith charged, were simply telling themselves that Negroes would be satisfied with segregation if they were provided with good housing, schools, health facilities, and jobs. These people were wrong because human beings have numerous needs beyond material things. She admitted that there were people who profited in various ways from segregation, but not always economically. The profiteers she described as follows: "The five major groups are the politicians; the mentally unstable who use 'the Negro' as an object on which to pour their hate and anxieties; real-estate owners and businessmen who make money from city ghettos and 'restricted areas'; a group of industrialists who use race prejudice to divide and weaken unions; and a few owners of large farms." On the matter of restrictive covenants, having to do with race or religion, Miss Smith said that it was prejudice which caused the price of real estate to go down and "not the fact that a Negro or Jewish family" moved into a community.

6. *Time*. The time for integration was now, she contended; and the Supreme Court had said as much. When each individual citizen began to change his own mental attitudes on segregation, what were considered to be problems would vanish. Segregation damaged everybody, particularly children; and each citizen and community had to waste no time in putting a stop to it.

7. *Reasoning After the Fact*. Unfair questions have been posed by unfair people regarding the inferiority of Negroes, their speech, their cleanliness, and their submission to the state of slavery. Again Miss Smith said that the Negro had suffered from poverty, hopelessness, lack of education, and unjust laws, all of which had contributed to his physical problems about which demagogues and ignorant white people complained. She pointed out that

in spite of the handicaps, many Negroes own beautiful homes; hundreds of thousands of individual Negroes possess as cultivated a mode of speech as one finds in this country; there are two hundred thousand college graduates who are Negro; there are women in the Negro race as sophisticated, as well traveled, as beautiful, and as exquisitely dressed as any women in the world. There are men of distinction, men who have achieved, men known across the earth for their intellectual and creative contributions to our world culture. This is common knowledge. It bears repeating.

8. *What Negroes Like*. In answer to those people who contended that Negroes liked to stay apart, to be with their own race, and would not want to give up their own churches and businesses, Miss Smith said that it was natural for sensitive people not to want to be mistreated in public or in private by the white race. They would, therefore, refrain from subjecting themselves to abuses until white people were prepared to respect their dignity. As for their churches, they were quite as admirable in ministerial eloquence and musical achievement as white churches. She thought that gradually more white people would be attending Negro churches than vice versa and that a similar transition would occur in businesses, with the clientele becoming mixed. The major change would be a sense of freedom from the tension of enforced segregation.

9. *Communism and Color*. Two questions were commonly raised under this heading. The first was why Americans should worry about what Communists thought since they lie about many things, including lynchings in the United States. Miss Smith's answer was that Communists have, indeed, used color and lynchings to their own advantage, but that the abolishment of legal segregation in the United States would bring about changes in the attitudes of Asians and Africans toward this country.

The second question had to do with the equating of American liberals with Communists because both groups oppose racial segregation. "Are not the liberals just following the Communist line?" was the question Miss Smith answered: "Long ago, Jesus Christ worked for peace. Does this make Him, now, a Communist? He also worked for brotherhood and for the acceptance of all people as children of God. Does this, now, place Him as the First Communist? It is a strange and sad thing to see many people who call themselves 'anti-Communists' credit communism with all the good, the creative and constructive beliefs and acts, which mankind has so laboriously achieved."

10. *Your Usefulness*. To those people who thought that "harm" came from speaking out against segregation and that the speaker would somehow lose his usefulness in the drive for integration, Lillian Smith answered that "words are powerful" in the cause of truth and justice, just as they may be powerful in the mouths of demagogues. If speaking in behalf of the integration of the races in the United States was not a "useful" thing to do because it was the sensible and just thing to do, then she had no vision of what might

be useful. She thought there was no point in hoarding one's use-fulness.

11. *Separate But Equal.* When asked "what is wrong about a 'separate but equal' way of life," Miss Smith rose to the occasion by explaining that people are not refrigerators or automobiles. She believed firmly that the psychological needs of human beings, in-volving esteem, recognition, acceptance, had not and could not be met in a segregated society. She spoke of a "growing climate" for children and the ideas of equality before God and before the law as essentials for the full development of the human being.

Now Is the Time concluded with a list of "Books You May Want to Read," compiled by Paula Snelling. The list included works of autobiography and fiction, books on segregation and human rights, Asia and Africa, psychology, sociology, philosophy, education, and history. A rather substantial reading list for the year 1955, it has continued to be useful.

Although there was change immediately in some areas of the South following the Supreme Court's decision on the public schools, there was rigid resistance in other areas. As a result various groups, under Negro leadership, were formed for the purpose of demanding and working for the citizenship rights of Negroes. Among the lead-ing groups to develop were the Congress of Racial Equality, the Student Non-Violent Coordinating Committee, and Dr. Martin Luther King's Southern Christian Leadership Conference. The National Association for the Advancement of Colored People had long been busy in the field of Negro rights and relationships, a fact which prompted Lillian Smith to dedicate her brief book, *Our Faces, Our Words,* to those leaders who had been working for many years and to the young people who had just begun to work.

Our Faces, Our Words, which was illustrated by photographs obtained from various news media, contained nine monologues purporting to represent the voices of as many people who had been affected by the sudden coming alive of the negro movements for civil rights. The final section of the book, called "The Day It Happens," was an essay giving Miss Smith's own views.

In "It's a terrible sleep when you can't wake up," the voice appeared to be that of a young Negro man who felt that he had been walking in a dream world or that he had been half asleep all his life until something had happened in the world of the American Negro that had aroused him and others toward activity on their own behalf. That brief monologue marked the beginning of Negro agitation, and it set the tone for others to speak.

Although the monologues were colored by Lillian Smith's ideas and beliefs, the author did, from time to time, catch the true quality of the speech of the character she was portraying. "We were there, man, and we knew we were there" was the heading of a monologue by another young Negro man who, while picketing a store, became aware for the first time that white people were actually seeing him.

"A cup of coffee" revealed how a young Negro college student, who had avoided involvement in racial concerns, came suddenly one afternoon to ask himself where his mother could get a cup of coffee if she happened to be downtown shopping and got tired. He realized not only that she would not be able to get a cup of coffee, but that she would not be able to go to a restroom either. When these truths came home to him, he had been reading J. D. Salinger's *Franny and Zooey* and listening with one ear to a friend talking about his mother's fainting down town because she could not sit down and have something to drink. This young man became active in the "sit-ins."

In that same monologue, the young speaker (all of the speakers are anonymous) recalled the training he had received from a representative of the Congress of Racial Equality which was advocating a nonviolent movement in which Negroes were expected to have compassion for white people. They were to hate evil, but not the people who perpetrated evil acts. These young people were advised to be wary, to be positive, but never to be reckless. Some of them, naturally, feared being considered cowards because they did not fight back; but the philosophy worked for the most part.

"The search for excellence takes us to strange places" is the monologue of a white girl who went to Mississippi to work in the civil rights movement. She said she was arrested for breaking a traffic rule, although she had broken none, and taken to jail where she was questioned in a vulgar way by the policeman about sexual relations with Negro men. This young speaker posed the same question Miss Smith had been asking for thirty years: "Why can't people change?"

In "What do we want?" Miss Smith portrayed a representative of the civil rights movement who spoke for both the whites and the Negroes who had been working together. When these mixed

124

groups of workers came into contact with white law officers, the officers appeared to be obsessed by the idea of sex between the races. Miss Smith's disgust with this obsession on the part of policemen prompted her to repeat what she had written in *Now Is the Time* that it was futile to speak of mongrelization of the races because "all human beings can breed with each other" as a matter of God's will, "but a man can't lay with his dog and bring forth a living creature." A main point here was that policemen, by their obsessive cruelty, were destroying the nonviolent movement, turning it into something else. The question was raised: "Why don't decent people say something?" Finally the question was answered as to what was wanted: dignity and the rights of a human being.

A Northern Negro, speaking in "Memories: how sweet and terrible!" also speaks with the voice of Lillian Smith as he refers to the ideas of Teilhard de Chardin that God is allowing man to create a culture beyond what is considered natural. This educated Negro from the North who went South to work with the Congress of Racial Equality found that he had little in common with the Southern Negroes for whom he was working. When he saw that many whites were on economic and cultural levels with many Negroes, he maintained that workers for civil rights must be willing to help poor whites as well as poor Negroes.

Through a fictional voice the reader of "You think about the three who were killed" hears the words Miss Smith had frequently used to describe the plight of poor whites in the South: their poverty of soul and culture. The voice is that of a white Southern minister who wishes he could tell the members of his church that, if they remain indifferent to the cause of civil rights, they must leave the church. He does not do so, of course; he does not do anything, because he would have no more than twenty members left if he cast out the indifferent. This minister calls the man who hates "dehumanized." In the first nine monologues, Miss Smith succeeded at intervals in submerging her ideas, words, and voice in order to approach the diction and vision of the characters she portrayed.

In "The day it happens," in which Lillian Smith is the speaker, she reviewed the beginnings of the nonviolent movement, mentioning the students who sat-in in Greensboro, North Carolina and in Montgomery, Alabama; Martin Luther King; and various other leaders. She said that little things sometimes led to major changes, citing Teilhard de Chardin on the matter of change on earth. In discussing the various kinds of deprivations Negroes in America have suffered, Miss Smith said again that families have been so deprived of food, clothing, shelter, health, education, and other necessities that their misery can be called "primitive." The misery had been so primitive and had gone on so long that the children found in city ghettos and other places were practically mute. These children, she thought, needed not food, but love. Miss Smith praised the nonviolent organizations for turning their attention to human relationships. She thought that the tutoring, the work with school dropouts, and other personal contacts between college students and young Negroes were steps in the right direction.

While agreeing that a kind of revolution was taking place in the United States, Miss Smith carefully pointed out that this was not a revolution against the country's political system but one in human relationships, a movement toward the protection of the rights of every individual citizen. She saw the Black Nationalist movement in the North as merely a new kind of slavery for the Negro, with no promise of freedom to those Negroes who took its cause. On the other hand, she said that human relations to some Southern senators meant only sex. She also deplored the violent intruders into the nonviolent movement, saying that they were filled with hate and were dangerous on any scene; but they were no more dangerous than ruthless white segregationists. Catastrophe could come to the United States, she concluded, unless the people are willing to face the future and use every resource to solve present problems.

According to a note in the front of *Our Faces, Our Words*, W. W. Norton & Company, Inc., the publisher, donated its profits to the Congress of Racial Equality. Miss Smith, though high in her praise of the same organization, gave warm support and approval to all of the nonviolent groups then working on human relations and civil rights problems. Thus her summary of the situation in 1964 posed a striking contrast to the lack of activity on the civil rights scene in 1936 when Lillian Smith and Paula Snelling began to publish their views in their own magazine.

CHAPTER 6

The Total Achievement

I *The Voice of Courage*

I N the thirty-year period, 1936 to 1966, Lillian Smith published seven books, a series of newspaper columns, a variety of articles for popular and literary magazines, and numerous book reviews. She also devoted about one and one-half years to the dramatization of *Strange Fruit*. Her total production would have been much greater, no doubt, if two very destructive fires had not resulted in the loss of her personal papers and several unpublished manuscripts. Among the papers destroyed were hundreds of letters, a novel set in China, notes on her travels to India, and two long fiction works set in the South. At the time of the present study, Miss Smith told the authors that she had a completed novel, *Julia*, in her bank safety box; but, because of its highly personal nature, she was unwilling for it to be read or published at this time. After 1953, Miss Smith was incapacitated from time to time by recurrent cancer, so that her writing time was reduced. Whether as a result of her physical suffering or as a natural development, her interests broadened through the years to include the whole man, his mental, physical, and social well-being, in a whole world which she visualized as being without racial barriers and governed democratically.

Had she written nothing but *Strange Fruit*, Lillian Smith would still have been a vital part of the American scene at mid-century. In that novel she championed an unpopular cause, integration of the races in the South; and she was deliberately sensational in doing so. If the average college freshman in 1971 has never heard of Lillian Smith and *Strange Fruit*, that simply indicates how great the changes have been in one generation. If that same freshman read the novel, he would surely want to know what all the fuss was about in Boston in 1944. Readers are now thoroughly familiar with Freud and his theories of sex; they know a good deal about miscegenation; and they have heard quite a lot about the Negro's right to full citizenship. It took courage, however, for a Southern white woman to speak out in 1944 against racial segregation, much less to publish a novel as Naturalistic in its composition as *Strange Fruit*. The fanfare was deafening, the financial rewards were great, and Miss Smith believed her literary achievement to be greater than it was.

In those early years of high fame and peak health, Miss Smith had a robust, Freudian attitude toward sex; and she shocked her female peers by chiding parents for repressing the natural urges of little children in such a way as to create guilt about sexual matters. In her nonfiction writings she relied heavily on her knowledge of psychoanalysis to try to stir her readers out of their lethargy. She wanted them, particularly Southerners, to see themselves as she (and Freud) saw them; and she seemed convinced that, once they had seen their reflections, they would surely want to change themselves. But, as she undoubtedly came to realize, people and societies change slowly, at their own pace, and for their own reasons. Even though she saw through the behavior of segregation-ists, demagogues, false preachers, Ku Klux Klanners, and Com-munists, and tried to heal them by showing them their reflections, nature was slow and change took its course, like a river gradually cutting a new channel.

Her second novel, *One Hour*, was a remarkable achievement for its sheer bulk, energy, and psychoanalytic conviction. It revealed her disgust with the McCarthy era witch-hunts and the foolishness of people who thrive on the persecution of others, but it was too preoccupied with the tortured analysis of what goes on in the minds of people and with the processes of guilt and sin. Miss Smith, being impatient with the slow way in which readers' minds work, became skilled at telling instead of showing the reader what her characters were up to. When David Landrum, the Episcopalian minister, seduces the wife of his best friend, the reader is revolted because Landrum knows so well what he is doing and why and then undertakes to rationalize what he has done. He is guilty, but he will keep on analyzing himself until he overcomes his guilt by finding something else or somebody else to blame.

Miss Smith's weakness as a novelist rested in her reliance upon other disciplines, including sociology, psychology, psychiatry, medicine, and theology for her interpretations of man. She had an excellent eye for physical details, and she was very successful in creating atmosphere by the use of these details. But her ideas of man, his motivations and behavior, were superimposed upon her pictorial details. She was adept at assembling her characters and the details of their lives, but she failed to let the characters reveal themselves as some other authors, such as William Faulkner or Flannery O'Connor, did. Assuming the role of the psychologist or sociologist, Miss Smith explained her characters to the reader. The reliance upon other disciplines for insight into human behavior took her away from her own insight and led her into obvious moralizing which is seldom successful in the short story or the novel. Miss Smith was not alone among contemporary writers in using this approach to fiction, but her persistence in its use amounts to a flaw in her novels.

II *The Voice of Experience*

Lillian Smith made a major contribution to the cause of racial reform because her voice rose out of personal experience. When it came to spotlighting and criticizing the South's deficiencies, she had firsthand knowledge which was not always available to her Northern counterparts. Only the Southern Negroes who were active in the liberal cause had more personal knowledge of the racial situation than Lillian Smith.

One positive achievement of Miss Smith's early work lay in the awakening she gave her Northern readers. People who had never lived in the South had a tendency to think of the region as "solid," with everybody residing there dedicated to racial segregation and to the subjugation of the Negro. That was never true, but it took Lillian Smith with her shock waves to prove it. She was always honest, sometimes using harsh and shocking language, in calling attention to what she saw as the social, psychological, and economic problems in the South.

As a joint founder and editor of *South Today*, she was responsible for what she called "the first liberal magazine" to be published in the South. At any rate, she maintained her freedom from coercion, which had often beset Southern liberals; and she made her voice heard through her own magazine. While there were other active white liberals in the South who were comforted by the presence of Miss Smith's little magazine, *South Today* served not only as a publishing outlet and as a means of contact between Southern liberals: it broke the barrier of silence between the South and the North, which exemplifies, in the final analysis, perhaps the outstanding contribution of Lillian Smith's life. As she moved within her region and between regions, she was the living message that the South had within its native population potential leaders for social reform.

On the other hand, Miss Smith's attacks upon every sacred aspect of Southern life, including such things as the tight community's pride in history and its reliance upon manners and traditions, served finally to reduce her contribution to active reform in the South. She saw racial segregation as the evil which overwhelmed everything else in the Southern community. The white Southerner's pride, self-respect, and sense of his own worth she attributed to his feeling of superiority because of his white skin. She was not on sound ground here, but she accepted her own idea so thoroughly that she refused to acknowledge many valuable and lasting characteristics of Southern life.

Louis D. Rubin, Jr., has written in *The Lasting South*[1] that family history and political and social history in the South were so intertwined early in this century that in a Southern town "the awareness of history is the *only* logical ordering device." Whereas Rubin thinks "It is the historical sense which in the South makes the individual identity, the sense of individuality possible," [2] Miss Smith placed another interpretation upon the Southerner's interest in history. Among other things, she saw this interest as false pride in a past era, an era of which she had never approved. Although Miss Smith frequently contended that man cannot understand the present or see into the future without considering his past, she was talking about his psychological and sociological past; and, in the view of numerous readers, she had not adequately considered the fact that these cannot, in the Southern region, be separated from family history and politics.

Her argument that Southerners are all mentally ill and that they are dehumanized into "mass man" only partially explains the people of her region, and her argument does not square with recent findings which describe the South as a modern stronghold of individualism in America. Her shock approach to solving the South's dilemma led her, therefore, to exaggerate some things and to ignore large areas of the Southern experience. It is true that she often referred, in her more reminiscent moods, to the importance of retaining what "was sweet and good" in her early life in the South, words which have little meaning unless she happened to be discussing her own family constellation and expressing her pride in the durability and resiliency of her grandparents, her parents, and the various Negroes associated with the family.

III *The Complex Personality*

With the publication of *Killers of the Dream*, Lillian Smith contributed to additional understanding between regions by analytically recounting her life in the South. What she had to say revealed the complexity of the conditioning which influences the adult behavor of the individual. Her candid self-study was a forerunner of the penchant, in the 1960's, for soul-searching, both publicly and privately. *Killers of the Dream*, as evidenced by the fact that it has become popular reading on college campuses and has become a valuable text, has served as a model for persons who seriously want to know why they feel and behave as they do.

When all is considered, it is obvious that one of Lillian Smith's greatest achievements lay in her portrayal of herself. Her collected writings amount to an extended biography, however much she may have tried to disguise herself in the printed page. What she wrote she believed, even though at various times she alienated segments of her following by writing as she believed. In other words, she proved herself to be one of those intransigent, Southern individualists of whom there are quite a few and who may yet save their region and themselves.

Notes and References

Chapter One

1. *Pseudopodia*, I (Fall, 1936), 6, 15.
2. Most of the personal information in this chapter is based upon an extensive file of notes which Miss Smith loaned to the authors and upon several hours of conversation between the authors and Miss Smith on June 25 and 26, 1965. Lillian Smith's five brothers were: Austin, Joe, DeWitt, Frank, and Wallace. Her sisters were Bertha, Annie Laurie, and Esther.
3. *Killers of the Dream* (New York, 1963), p. 20.

Chapter Two

1. *Pseudopodia*, I, 1 (Spring, 1936). Since the pages of the first issue of *Pseudopodia* are not numbered, references are made only to volume and issue number.
2. *Ibid.*
3. John D. Allen, "Southern Agrarianism: Revised Version," *Pseudopodia*, I (Summer, 1936), 14.
4. *Pseudopodia*, I (Fall, 1936), 6, 15.
5. *Ibid.*, p. 6.
6. *Ibid.*
7. *Ibid.*
8. *Ibid.*, p. 15.
9. *Saturday Review* (December 24, 1960), pp. 18-19.
10. *The Chicago Tribune Books Today* (June 6, 1965), p. 5.
11. Chris Eckl, "An Artist Cannot Hate," *Atlanta Journal* (April 24, 1966), p. 2-B.
12. W. J. Cash, "The Reign of the Commonplace," *Pseudopodia*, I (*Fall, 1936*).
13. *Pseudopodia*, I, 1 (Fall, 1936), 8.
14. *Ibid.*, I (Winter, 1937), 7.
15. *The North Georgia Review*, II (Winter, 1937-38), 16-19, 31-32.
16. *Ibid.*, p. 16.
17. *Ibid.*, p. 31.
18. *Ibid.*, III (Summer, 1938), 7-12.
19. *Ibid.*, p. 7.

20. *Ibid.*, III (Fall and Winter, 1938-39), 12-15.
21. *Ibid.*, p. 14.
22. Eckl, "An Artist Cannot Hate." p. 2-B.
23. *South Today*, VII (Spring, 1942), 30.

Chapter Three

1. *Publishers Weekly* (May 27, 1944), p. 1998, and (June 10, 1944), p. 2169.
2. *Ibid.* (April 1, 1944), pp. 1289-90, and (April 8, 1944), p. 1443.
3. Struthers Burt, "The Making of a New South," *Saturday Review* (March 11, 1944), p. 10.
4. Bernard DeVoto, "The Easy Chair," *Harper's* (May, 1944), p. 525.
5. Orville Prescott, "Outstanding Novels," *Yale Review*, XXXIII (Spring, 1944), x.
6. Joseph McSorley, "Strange Fruit," *Catholic World* (May, 1944), p. 182.
7. Cecelia Gaul, "Strange Fruit," *Christian Century* (July 19, 1944), p. 854.
8. M.W., "*Strange Fruit*," *Christian Science Monitor* (May 1, 1944), p. 14.
9. Edward Weeks, "Strange Fruit," *Atlantic* (May, 1944), p. 127.
10. Fred H. Marcus, "*Cry, the Beloved Country and Strange Fruit*: Exploring Man's Inhumanity to Man," *English Journal* (December, 1962), p. 609.
11. Francis Downing, "Strange Fruit," *Commonweal* (April 7, 1944), p. 626.
12. Background information based upon notes provided by Miss Smith.
13. The Library of Congress has no copy of the play, *Strange Fruit*.
14. Rosamond Gilder, "Matter and Art," *Theatre Arts* (February, 1946), p. 73.
15. Stark Young, "*Strange Fruit*, Etc.," *New Republic*, CXIII (December 17, 1945), 839.
16. George Jean Nathan, *The Theater Book of the Year 1945-46: A Record and an Interpretation* (New York, 1946), p. 215.
17. Gilder, pp. 73-74.
18. Nathan, pp. 212-13.
19. Gilder, p. 74.

Chapter Four

1. *South Today*, IX (Winter, 1945), 5.
2. *North Georgia Review*, V (Winter, 1940-41), 8.

3. Edmund Fuller, "Sins and Sorrows," *Saturday Review* (October 3, 1959), p. 22.

4. *Ibid.*

5. Paul West, *"One Hour" New Statesman* (May 28, 1960), p. 799.

6. "Books," *New Yorker* (September 26, 1959), p. 191.

Chapter Five

1. Miss Smith's column, "A Southerner Talking," began October 23, 1948, and terminated on September 3, 1949.

2. Stanley Edgar Hyman, *Flannery O'Connor* (Minneapolis, 1966), p. 43.

3. *The New Republic* (September 18, 1944), pp. 331-33.

4. Edmund Rucker, "How to Work for Racial Equality," *New Republic* (July 2, 1945), p. 23.

5. *New Republic* (July 2, 1945), pp. 23-24.

6. *New Republic* (December 16, 1957), pp. 12-16.

7. *Black, White and Gray*, ed. Bradford Daniel (New York, 1964), p. 266.

8. *Saturday Review* (October 2, 1965), pp. 20-35.

9. *Redbook* (May, 1961), pp. 44-45.

10 *Redbook* (August, 1962), p. 96.

11. *Ibid.*

12. *New South*, (Winter, 1966), pp. 64-66.

13. "A Strange Kind of Love," *Saturday Review* (October 20, 1962), pp. 18-20, 27.

14. Frank Daniel, "Miss Smith Looks to the Future," *Atlanta Journal* (November 22, 1964), p. 1-C.

15. Chris Eckl, "An Artist Cannot Hate," *Atlanta Journal* (April 24, 1966), p. 2-B.

16. *Chicago Tribune Books Today* (March 13, 1966), p. 1.

17. *Ibid.* (June 6, 1965), p. 5.

18. *Ibid.* (April 10, 1966), p. 8.

19. *Ibid.* (March 22, 1964), p. 3.

20. *Ibid.* (October 18, 1964), p. 4.

21. *Ibid.* (May 8, 1966), p. 11.

22. *Saturday Review* (September 20, 1958), p. 21.

23. *Ibid.* (September 7, 1963), pp. 19-20.

24. *Ibid.* (August 25, 1962), p. 24.

Chapter Six

1. Louis D. Rubin, Jr., "An Image of the South," *The Lasting South*, ed. Louis D. Rubin, Jr., and James Jackson Kilpatrick (Chicago, 1957), p. 5.

2. *Ibid.*

Selected Bibliography

PRIMARY SOURCES

1. Books

Strange Fruit. New York: Reynal & Hitchcock, 1944.
Killers of the Dream. New York: W.W. Norton & Co., Inc., 1949.
The Journey. Cleveland: The World Publishing Co., 1954.
Now Is the Time. New York: The Viking Press, 1955.
One Hour. New York: Harcourt, Brace & World, Inc., 1959.
Memory of a Large Christmas. New York: W.W. Norton & Co., Inc. 1962.
Our Faces, Our Words. New York: W.W. Norton & Co., Inc., 1964.

2. *Articles in Periodicals*

A. In *Pseudopodia*

"The Harris Children's Town—Maxwell, Ga.," I (Spring, 1936), 4-8.
"Dope with Lime," *ibid.*, p. 12.
"Big Granny," *ibid.*, I (Summer, 1936), 4-5, 15-16.
"An Open Letter to Mr. Caldwell on Child Care," an unsigned editorial, *ibid.*, p. 8.
"Dope with Lime," *ibid.*, p. 12.
"One More Sigh for the Good Old South," I (Fall, 1936), 6, 15.
"From Lack of Understanding," an unsigned editorial, *ibid.*, pp. 8, 9.
"Dope with Lime," *ibid.*, p. 12.
"Book Reviews," *ibid.*, pp. 13-14.
"Mountain Monotones: Jabe's Mule," I (Winter, 1937), 5, 6, 20.
"Out of the Gulf Stream," *ibid.*, pp. 7, 11.

B. In *The North Georgia Review*

"Along Their Way," II (Spring, 1937), 3-4.
"Book Review," *ibid.*, pp. 20-21.
"Dope with Lime," *ibid.*, p. 23.
"Dope with Lime," II (Summer, 1937), 2.
"The Artist in Society," *ibid.*, p. 11.
"Book Reviews," *ibid.*, p. 21.
"Wisdom Crieth in the Streets," III (Fall, 1937), 1-3.
"Book Reviews," *ibid.*, p. 23.

"Dope with Lime," II (Winter, 1937-38), 2.
"Exegesis," *ibid.*, p. 5.
"He That Is without Sin," *ibid.*, pp. 16-19, 31-32.
"Book Reviews," *ibid.*, pp. 26-29.
"Dope with Lime," III (Spring, 1938), 2.
"Act of Penance," *ibid.*, p. 21.
"And the Waters Flow On," III (Summer, 1938), 7-12.
"Wanted: Lessons in Hate," III (Fall and Winter, 1938-39), 12-15.
"Two Sketches," *ibid.*, p. 19.
"Dope with Lime," IV (Spring, 1939), 2.
"Out of the Gulf Stream: Southern Fiction," *Ibid.*, pp. 24-29.
"Dope with Lime," IV (Autumn, 1939), 4.
"Behind the Drums," *ibid.*, p. 12.
"Dope with Lime," IV (Winter, 1939-40), 4.
"So You're Seeing the South," *ibid.*, pp. 18-22.
"Dope with Lime," V (Spring, 1940), 4.
"Figs and Doodle Bugs: A Story," *ibid.*, pp. 15-21.
"Southern Conference," an editorial, *ibid.*, pp. 23-26.
"Dope with Lime," V (Summer, 1940), p. 4.
"In Defense of Life," *ibid.*, p. 11.
"Dope with Lime," V (Winter, 1940-41), 4.
"An Essay into Internationalism: Of Epicycles and Men," written jointly with Paula Snelling, *ibid.*, pp. 9-17.
"Jordan Is so Chilly," *ibid.*, pp. 31-43.
"Dope with Lime," VI (Winter, 1941), 4.
"Man Born of Woman," written jointly with Paula Snelling, *ibid.*, pp. 7-17.
"Paw and the Rest of Us," *ibid.*, pp. 39-45.

C. In *South Today*

"Dope with Lime," VII (Spring, 1942), 4.
"Portrait of the Deep South Speaking to Negroes on Morale," *ibid.*, pp. 34-37.
"Dope with Lime," VII (Autumn-Winter, 1942-43), 4.
"Buying a New World with Old Confederate Bills," unsigned, *ibid.*, pp. 7-30.
"Addressed to Intelligent White Southerners," *ibid.*, pp. 34-43.
"Dope with Lime," VII (Spring, 1943), 4.
"Two Men and a Bargain," *ibid.*, pp. 5-14.
"Georgia Primer," *ibid.*, pp. 29-32.
"Dope with Lime," VIII (Spring-Summer, 1944), 4.
"Today's Children and Their Tomorrow," unsigned, *ibid.*, p. 9.
"Growing Plays," *ibid.*, pp. 32-60.
"Putting Away Childish Things," *ibid.*, pp. 61-66.

Selected Bibliography

D. Miscellaneous Periodicals

"Address to White Liberals," *New Republic*, CXI (September 18, 1944), 331-33. Reprinted in *Primer for White Folks*, ed. Bucklin Moon. Garden City, N.Y.: Doubleday, Doran and Co., Inc., 1945, pp. 484-87.

"Personal History of *Strange Fruit*," *Saturday Review*, XXVIII (February 17, 1945), 9-10.

"How to Work for Racial Equality," *New Republic*, CXIII (July 2, 1945), 23-24.

"It's Growing Time in Georgia," *The Nation*, CLXIII (July 13, 1946), 34-36.

"The Right to Grow," *Womans' Home Companion*, LXX (October, 1946), 25.

"Pay Day in Georgia," *The Nation*, CLXIV (February 1, 1947), 118-19.

"Postscript to Pay Day," a letter to the editor, *The Nation*, CLXIV (February 22, 1947), 231.

"Walls of Segregation Are Crumbling," *New York Times Magazine* (July 15, 1951), p. 9.

"Ten Years from Today," *Vital Speeches*, XVII (August 15, 1951), 669-72.

"Declaration of Faith in America," *New York Times Magazine* (September 21, 1952), p. 13.

"Prayer for a Better World," *Parents Magazine*, XXX (December, 199), 108.

"Right Way Is Not a Moderate Way," *Phylon*, XVII (December, 1956), 335-41.

"Winner Names the Age," *Phylon*, XVIII (October, 1957), 203-12.

"No Easy Way, Now," *New Republic*, CXXVII (December 16, 1957), 12-16.

"And Suddenly Something Happened," *Saturday Review*, XLI (September 20, 1958), 21.

"Novelists Need a Commitment," *Saturday Review*, XLIII (December 24, 1960), 18-19.

"Ordeal of Southern Women," *Redbook*, CXVII (May, 1961), 44-45.

"School Play: Choice of Play," *English*, XIII (Spring, 1961), 139-40. (Written jointly with her sister and signed L. E. Smith and J. E. Smith).

"An Awakening of the Heart," *Redbook*, CXIX (August, 1962), 27, 96.

"No More Ladies in the Dark," *Saturday Review*, XLV (August 25, 1962), 24.

"Now. The Lonely Decision for Right or for Wrong." *Life*, LIII (October 12, 1962), 44.

"A Strange Kind of Love," *Saturday Review*, XLV (October 20, 1962), 18-20, 94.

"Introduction," *Freedom Ride* by James Peck. New York: Simon and Schuster, 1962, pp. 9-13.

"Too Tame the Shrew," *Saturday Review*, XLVI (February 23, 1963), 34, 44.

"Thoughts as Her Travels Ended," *Saturday Review*, XLVI (September 7, 1963), 19-20.

"The Mob and the Ghost," *The Progressive* (December, 1962). (Reprinted in *Black, White and Gray*, ed. Bradford Daniel. (New York: Sheed and Ward, 1964), pp. 266-77.

"The Day It Happens to Each of Us," *McCall's*. XCII (November, 1964), 124-25, 166, 168. (This is an excerpt from *Our Faces, Our Words*.)

"Poets Among the Demagogues," *Saturday Review*, XLVIII (October 2, 1965), 20, 35.

"Acceptance Speech for the Charles S. Johnson Award, 1966," *23rd Annual Institute of Race Relations*. Nashville: Fisk University, 1966, pp. 3-4.

"Miss Smith on SNCC," *New South*, XXI (Winter, 1966), 64-66. (Reprinted from *The Atlanta Constitution*, January 14, 1966. This was a "Letter to the Editor," which appeared originally under the title "Old Dream, New Killers.")

3. Articles in Newspapers

A. Book Reviews in *Chicago Tribune Books Today*

"Reapers of the Whirlwind," a review of *The Keepers of the House* by Shirley Ann Grau, March 22, 1964, p. 3.

"The South on the Couch," a review of *The Southern Mystique* by Howard Zinn, October 18, 1964, p. 4.

"Facets of the South," a review of *Many Thousands Gone* by Ronald L. Fair, February 21, 1965, p. 5.

"With a Wry Smile Hovering Over All," a review of *Everything That Rises Must Converge* by Flannery O'Connor, June 6, 1965, p. 5.

"The Post War South," a review of *The South as It Is*, 1865-66, a report by John Richard Dennett, edited by Henry M. Christman, July 11, 1965, p. 8.

"Speaking to the Human Condition," a review of *The Ignoble Savages* by Mariano Picon-Salas, August 22, 1965, p. 8.

"Budding Genius of a Priest," a review of *The Making of a Mind* by Theilhard de Chardin, October 31, 1965, p. 12.

"Savoring a Distant Experience," a review of *La Bâtarde* by Violette Leduc, October 31, 1965, p. 10.

"Defending a Thinker and Poet," a review of *Teilhard de Chardin: The Man and His Meaning* by Henri de Lubac, S.J., November 28, 1965, p. 6.

"Truths about Human Beings," a review of *Swans on an Autumn River* by Sylvia Townsend Warner, February 13, 1966, p. 6.

"An Optimist Looks at the Human Race," a review of *The Appearance of Man* by Pierre Teilhard de Chardin, March 13, 1966, p. 1.

Selected Bibliography

"A Search for Reality," a review of *The Far Family* by Wilma Dykeman, March 20, 1966, p. 6.

"Magic Mixed with Truth," a review of *Greenstone* by Sylvia Ashton-Warner, March 27, 1966, p. 9.

"Glimpse of a Southern Writer," a review of *The Ballad* of *Carson McCullers* by Oliver Evans, April 10, 1966, p. 8.

"Walk on a Swinging Bridge," a review of *Southerner* by Charles L. Weltner, May 8, 1966, p. 11.

"Captive of One's Own Space-Making," a review of *The Hidden Dimension* by Edward T. Hall, June 26, 1966, p. 13.

B. Regular Column in *The Chicago Defender*

"A Southerner Talking": October 16, 1948, pp. 16, 7; October 20, 1948, p. 16; October 23, 1948, p. 16; October 27, 1948, p. 16. November 6, 1948, p. 16; November 13, 1948, p. 16. December 4, 1948, p. 16; December 11, 1948, p. 16; December 18, 1948, p. 16; December 25, 1948, p. 16. January 1, 1949, p. 16; January 8, 1949, p. 16; January 15, 1949, p. 16; January 22, 1949, p. 16; January 29, 1949, p. 16. February 5, 1949, p. 16; February 12, 1949, p. 16; February 19, 1949, p. 16; February 26, 1949, p. 16. March 5, 1949, p. 16; March 12, 1949, p. 16; March 19, 1949, p. 16; March 26, 1949, p. 16. April 2, 1949, p. 16; April 9, 1949, p. 16; April 16, 1949, p. 16; April 23, 1949, p. 16; April 30, 1949, p. 16. May 7, 1949, p. 16; May 14, 1949, p. 16; May 21, 1949, p. 16; May 28, 1949, p. 16. June 4, 1949, p. 16; June 11, 1949, p. 16; June 18, 1949, p. 16; June 25, 1949, p. 16. July 2, 1949, p. 16; July 9, 1949, p. 16; July 16, 1949, p. 16; July 23, 1949, p. 16. August 6, 1949, p. 16; August 13, 1949, p. 16; August 20, 1949, p. 16; August 27, 1949, p. 16. September 3, 1949, p. 16.

SECONDARY SOURCES

1. General Articles

FARNHAM, MARYNIA F. "The Pen and the Distaff," *Saturday Review*, XXX (February 22, 1947), 7-8, 29-30. Compares Lillian Smith with Ayn Rand and other female writers.

GRAFTON, SAM. "We're Mighty Fond of Our Miss Lil," *Colliers*, LXXV (January 28, 1950), 28-29, 58-59. Discusses the friendliness of the people in Clayton, Georgia, toward Lillian Smith.

JACK, HOMER A. "Lillian Smith of Clayton, Georgia," *Christian Century*, LXXIV (October 2, 1957), 1166-68. Recounts a visit to Lillian Smith's home on Old Screamer Mountain just before her completion of *One Hour*.

LEONARD, GEORGE B. "Not Black Power, but Human Power," an interview with Lillian Smith, *Look*, XXX (September 6, 1966), 40, 42-43. Reports Miss Smith's views on race relations as she gave them from her hospital bed a few weeks before her death.

MARCUS, FRED H. "*Cry, the Beloved Country and Strange Fruit:* Exploring Man's Inhumanity to Man," *English Journal*, LI (December, 1962), 609-16. Sees *Cry the Beloved Country* as ending on a note of optimism, while *Strange Fruit* ends on "an ironic note, an irony devoid of humor."

"Miss Lil," three letters to the editor, *Colliers* LXXV (March 18, 1950, 6. Responses of neighbors in Clayton, Georgia, to the article by Sam Grafton (see above).

MOORE, EUGENE. "Illness Plagues 4 Georgia Writers," *The Atlanta Journal and Constitution*, August 15, 1965, p. 6. Discusses the poor health of Lillian Smith, Edison Marshall, Carson McCullers, and Caroline Miller.

MOREHOUSE, LETTY. "Bio-Bibliography of Miss Lillian Smith." Unpublished graduate paper, Florida State University, 1956. Outlines the author's life and works.

REEVES, PASCHAL. "Lillian Smith (1897-1966), *A Bibliographical Guide to the Study of Southern Literature*. ed. Louis D. Rubin, Jr. Baton Rouge: Louisiana State University Press, 1969. Gives a brief summary of Miss Smith's work.

ROSTAD, PAL OLAV. "Lillian Smith and the Race Problem." Unpublished thesis, The University of Oslo, 1969. Concludes that Miss Smith helped prepare the way for SNCC and other Negro civil rights organizations.

"SMITH, LILLIAN (EUGENIA) 1897—," *Current Biography*. New York: H. W. Wilson Co., 1945. Includes a biographical sketch up to the publication of *Strange Fruit*.

2. Significant Reviews of *Strange Fruit*

BURGUM, EDWIN BERRY. "Sociological Pattern of Strange Fruit," *Science and Society*, IX (Winter, 1945), 77-82. States that "the novel is far in advance of those radicals who oppose racial discrimination without advocating racial admixture."

BURT, STRUTHERS. "The Making of a New South," *Saturday Review*, XXVII (March 11, 1944), 10. Calls the book a major novel.

COWLEY, MALCOLM. "Southways," *New Republic*, CX (March 6, 1944), 320-22. Praises the novel for its social attacks.

DEVOTO, BERNARD. "The Easy Chair," *Harper's Magazine*, CLXXXVIII (May, 1944), 525-28. Calls it a courageous novel.

DOWNING, FRANCIS. "Strange Fruit," *Commonweal*, XXXIX (April 7, 1944), 626. Concludes that the novel does not succeed because the author seems to have the idea that a change of symbols will solve man's problems.

Selected Bibliography

"Feverish Fascination," *Time*, XLIII (March 20, 1944), 99-100, 102. Concludes that the novel has a melodramatic fascination, although the characters are like prisoners who do not struggle.

Gaul, Cecelia. "Strange Fruit," *Christian Century*, LXI (July 19,1944), p. 854. Calls this a good novel with an annoying style.

McSorley, Joseph. "*Strange Fruit*," *Catholic World*, CLIX (May, 1944), 182. Calls the story "unfit for general circulation."

M. W. "*Strange Fruit*," *Christian Science Monitor* (May 1, 1944), p. 14. Calls the novel an earnest effort, but criticizes the speech and behavior of its characters.

Prescott, Orville. "Outstanding Novels," *Yale Review*, XXXIII (Spring, 1944), x. Praises the novel for its moving depiction of Negroes and for its style.

Trilling, Diana. "Fiction in Review," *The Nation*, CLVIII (March 18, 1944), 342. Discusses *Strange Fruit* as a very good problem novel.

Weeks, Edward. "Strange Fruit," *The Atlantic*, CLXXIII (Mary, 1944), 127. Finds the book shocking but not pornographic.

3. Articles in *Publishers Weekly* (arranged chronologically)

"*Strange Fruit* Banned by Boston Booksellers," CXLV (March 25, 1944), 1289-90. Reports on the original banning of the book by the booksellers as a result of complaints registered with the Police Department.

"Tips from the Publishers," CXLV (April 1, 1944), 1369. Reports that the publishers of *Strange Fruit* claim that 50,000 copies of the book had been sold as of March 27, 1944.

"Censorship a Local Problem," an editorial by Frederic G. Melcher, CXLV (April 8, 1944), 1443. Criticizes the local banning of *Strange Fruit* because it contains a "a four-letter word."

"DeVoto and Isenstadt on Trial in *Strange Fruit* Case," CXLV (April 15, 1944), 1527. Reports that the trial of the two accused was postponed from April 12 to April 26.

"Cambridge Bookseller Fined for Selling *Strange Fruit*," CXLV (May 6, 1944), 1768. Reports that charges were dropped against DeVoto, while Isenstadt was fined $100.00 for selling the book and $100.00 for having obscene literature in his possession. Isenstadt appealed the case.

"*Strange Fruit* Banned, Then Released by Post Office," CXLV (May 20, 1944), 1922-23. Reports on the banning and lifting of the ban by the New York post office.

"*Strange Fruit* Banned in Detroit 'by Gentlemen's Agreement,' " CXLV (May 27, 1944), 1998-99. Relates the action of the United Automobile Workers' Union Book Shop in resisting the ban.

"Detroit Public Library and the *Strange Fruit* Case," a letter to the editor by Ralph A. Ulveling, CXLV (June 10, 1944), 2169. Explains stand taken by the Detroit Public Library to prevent official banning of the book.

"Publishers Weekly—Ad Club Award Goes to Reynal and Hitchcock for *Strange Fruit* Campaign," CXLVII (March 10, 1945), 1110-113. Praises the dignified advertising campaign for *Strange Fruit*, a book with sensational subject matter.

"Hearing on Appeal in *Strange Fruit* Case," CXLVII (May 12, 1945), 1916. Reports that a hearing was held but no decision was reached.

"Massachusetts Supreme Court Upholds *Strange Fruit* Ban," CXLVIII (September 29, 1945), 1547-48. Reports that a majority of the court upheld Isenstadt's conviction on both counts.

"DeVoto Issues Statement Against *Strange Fruit* Decision," CXLVIII (October 6, 1945), 1664. Reports that DeVoto said the Court made its decision on narrow legalistic grounds without considering the social issues raised by the case.

"The Decision in the Strange Fruit Case," by Harold Williams, CXLVIII (October 20, 1945), 1831-32. Criticizes as unsound the process by which the Supreme Judicial Court of Massachusetts made its decision.

4. Additional Articles on the Banning of *Strange Fruit*

"Books: Miscegenation," *Newsweek*, XXIII (May 29, 1944), 72. Reviews the steps taken by the United States Post Office in banning and then lifting the ban on *Strange Fruit*.

DEVOTO, BERNARD. "The Decision in the *Strange Fruit* Case: The Obscenity Statute in Massachusetts," *New England Quarterly*, XIX (June, 1946), 147-83. Reviews the incidents of the case, pointing out that the Civil Liberties Union decided to instigate the case to "end the extralegal censorship" and force public officials to take a stand.

———. "The Easy Chair," *Harper's Magazine*, CLXXXIX (June, 1944), 148-51. Tells of his and Isenstadt's arrest for buying and selling *Strange Fruit* in the presence of a policeman.

———. "The Easy Chair," *Harper's Magazine*, CXC (February, 1945), 224-28. Praises the "high artistic excellence" of *Strange Fruit* and criticizes the State of Massachusetts for suppression of literary works.

———. "The Easy Chair," *Harper's Magazine*, CXCI (December, 1945), 505-8. Reviews events leading up to the decision of the Supreme Judicial Court of Massachusetts in the *Strange Fruit* case.

LERNER, MAX. "On Lynching a Book," *Public Journal*. New York: Viking Press, 1945, p. 131-34. (Reprinted in *The First Freedom*, ed. Robert B. Downs. Chicago: American Library Association, 1960, pp. 209-10.) Protests the "Messy effort to suppress Lillian Smith's novel."

5. Significant Reviews of the play, *Strange Fruit*
    GIBBS, WOLCOTT. "The Theatre," *The New Yorker*, XXI (December 8, 1945), 54. Praises the play for its emotional depth while charging that its structure is faulty.
    GILDER, ROSAMOND. "Matter and Art," *Theatre Arts*, XXX (February, 1946), 73-75. Calls the play a "series of dialogues rather than a march of events."
    NATHAN, GEORGE JEAN. "Strange Fruit." *Theatre Book of the Year, 1945-1946*. New York: A.A. Knopf, 1946. Calls the play a melodrama with monotonous staging.
    "*Strange Fruit*," *Life*, XIX (December 24, 1945), 33-35. Concludes that the author explains too much and dramatizes too little.
    "*Strange Fruit*," *Time*, XLVI (December 10, 1945), 77. States that Miss Smith was unable to transfer her material from one form to another, calling her an "unconverted novelist."
    "Strange Fruition," Newsweek, XXVI (December 10, 1945), 92-93. Concludes that even though some scenes are deeply moving, the authors followed the novel too closely for dramatic success.
    YOUNG, STARK. "*Strange Fruit*, Etc., "*New Republic* CXIII (December 17, 1945), 839. Compares *Strange Fruit* with *Deep Are the Roots*, concluding that *Strange Fruit* is "truer to the South," but that *Deep Are the Roots* is better stagecraft.

6. Significant Reviews of *Killers of the Dream*
    BARRETT, WILLIAM G. "*Killers of the Dream*," *Psychoanalytic Quarterly*, XX (January, 1951), 129-30. Praises the book for its honesty.
    FARIS, ELLSWORTH. "Sin, Sex and Segregation," *Christian Century*, LXVI (December, 1949), 1457. Calls the book a highly exaggerated portrayal of what the South is like.
    GRIFFIN, JOHN HOWARD. "Again, Lillian Smith's South," *Southwest Review*, XLVII (Winter, 1962), 97-98. Comments on the republication of the book and praises it as "a highly original work of art."
    KERLIN, ROBERT T. "A Broadcast on *Killers of the Dream*," *The Negro History Bulletin*, XIII (February, 1950), 117-18. Concludes that this book has a solemn and weighty message for the American people.
    MOON, BUCKLIN. "Killers of the Dream," *New York Times Book Review* (October 23, 1949), p. 3. Gives a useful discussion of the author's successes and failures in this book.
    RAINEY, H. P. "The Mind of the South," *Saturday Review*, XXX (October 22, 1949), 21-22. Praises the author for her honesty in searching her own soul.
    "Tract from the South," *Time*, LIV (October 31, 1949), 82-83, 86. Calls the book "badly organized" and repetitive, although it contains some valuable insights.

7. Significant Reviews of *The Journey*

LYNCH, W. S. "A Modern Pilgrim," *Saturday Review*, XXXVII (May 15, 1954), 11. Praises the author for her analysis of the age in which she is writing.

ROLO, CHARLES J. "Reader's Choice," *The Atlantic*, CXCIII (May, 1954), 80. Regards the book as a "testimony to the dignity of man," written with a "deep sense of life's complexity."

8. Significant Reviews of *Now Is the Time*

BRUNN, R. R. "Now Is the Time," *Christian Science Monitor*, (February 10, 1955), p. 9. Calls attention to the author's desire to end segregation with reason, not emotion.

CARTER, HODDING. "Hope in the South," *Saturday Review*, XXXVIII (April 2, 1955), 29, 35. Praises the succinctness with which the author presents the major challenges concerning racial equality.

GILL, T. A. "Alibis Unmasked," *Christian Century*, LXXII (August 24, 1955), 973. Calls the book a "smart woman's trumpet blast."

McGILL, RALPH. "A Matter of Change," *The New York Times Book Review*, February 13, 1955, p. 7. Praises the book, despite the dogmatism of the author.

ROSS, MARY. "Lillian Smith on Segregation," *New York Herald Tribune Book Review*, February 13, 1955, p. 4. States that the book can help Americans find out how to solve the race problem.

9. Significant Reviews of *One Hour*

FEIDLER, L. A. "Decency Is Not Enough," *New Republic*, CXLII (January 4, 1960), 15-16. Calls the book exemplary because it punctures middlebrow piety of its time.

FULLER, EDMUND. "Sins and Sorrows," *Saturday Review*, XLII (October 3, 1959), 22. Concludes that Miss Smith undertook too much and did not succeed in this novel.

ROLO, CHARLES J. "Reader's Choice," *The Atlantic*, CCIV (November, 1959), 180-81. Discusses the book's insight and sensitivity.

WEST, PAUL. "*One Hour*," *New Statesman* (May 28, 1960), p. 799. Criticizes the author's choice of narrator, while praising the total effect as profound and fluent.

10. Obituaries

BROCKWAY, GEORGE P. "You Do It Because You Love Somebody," *Saturday Review*, XLIX (October 22, 1966), 53-54. Cites Lillian Smith as "a master of four genres—the novel, the parable, the essay, and the oration."

Selected Bibliography

"Deaths of Note: Lillian Smith, Controversial Dixie Author," *St. Petersburg Times*, September 29, 1966, p. 11-A. Cites Miss Smith as a champion of civil rights.

"LILLIAN SMITH," *Publishers Weekly*, CXC (October 10, 1966), 53-54. Recounts Miss Smith's twenty-four years as a writer and leader for racial equality.

LONG, MARGARET. "The Sense of Her Presence: A Memorial for Lillian Smith," *New South*, XXI (Fall, 1966), 71-77. Describes Miss Smith's funeral and recalls the high spots of her life.

MOORE, EUGENE. "Georgia Writer Fought Long Against Bigotry," *The Atlanta Journal*, September 29, 1968, p. 18-D. Commemorates the second anniversary of Lillian Smith's death.

"One Less Friend in Georgia," an unsigned editorial,*Christian Century*, LXXXIII (October 12, 1966), 1234. Reviews Miss Smith's work, calling *Strange Fruit* a social banner rather than a literary masterpiece.

"The South: Herald of the Dream," *Time*, LXXXVIII (October 7, 1966), 36-37. Reviews Miss Smith's life and cites her disillusionment in 1966 with the Congress of Racial Equality.

Index

Index